THE ROAD LESS WORN

The Road *Less* Worn

**HOW TO BE YOURSELF
IN A WORLD THAT WANTS YOU
TO BE SOMEONE ELSE**

Erin Flynn

WREN HOUSE *press*

COPYRIGHT © 2025 ERIN FLYNN
All rights reserved.

THE ROAD LESS WORN
How to Be Yourself in a World That Wants You to Be Someone Else
First Edition

ISBN	978-1-967115-04-4	*Hardcover*
	978-1-967115-06-8	*Paperback*
	978-1-967115-05-1	*Ebook*
	978-1-967115-07-5	*Audiobook*

LCCN 2025908273

For Colin—I can venture into the unknown because you are the steady anchor that grounds me.

For Rooney—May you travel down the road less worn, knowing you're deeply loved and never alone.

CONTENTS

Preface: The Edit xiii
Introduction: The Stories We Carry xxv

PART ONE Culture: What We Never Thought to Question 1
PART TWO Clutter: Letting Go of What Doesn't Fit 53
PART THREE Curating: Making Space for What Fits 105
PART FOUR Capsule Living: Creating Your Own Way 139
PART FIVE The Road Ahead: A Freer, More Beautiful Way to Live 199

Afterword: Your Compass 223
Acknowledgments 235
About the Author 239
About Cladwell 241

THE ROAD NOT TAKEN
by ROBERT FROST

Two roads diverged in a yellow wood,
And sorry I could not travel both
And be one traveler, long I stood
And looked down one as far as I could
To where it bent in the undergrowth;

Then took the other, as just as fair,
And having perhaps the better claim,
Because it was grassy and wanted wear;
Though as for that the passing there
Had worn them really about the same,

And both that morning equally lay
In leaves no step had trodden black.
Oh, I kept the first for another day!
Yet knowing how way leads on to way,
I doubted if I should ever come back.

I shall be telling this with a sigh
Somewhere ages and ages hence:
Two roads diverged in a wood, and I—
I took the one less traveled by,
And that has made all the difference.

PREFACE
The Edit

This is a story about decluttering, but not in the way you might expect. You won't find any tips for minimalist living or how to organize your drawers here. This is about decluttering my life, by digging deep into the stories I used to tell myself about what a "good life" was supposed to look like. I discovered that much of what filled my days was there because someone else said it should be, not because it brought me joy or felt true to who I am. It has taken work to clear out what I was holding on to, to rediscover a life I loved living.

It's a story that started unexpectedly in my closet. Amid a sea of 450 clothing items scattered across my bedroom floor—stacks of nearly identical striped shirts, a pile of jeans that no longer fit, dresses with tags still attached—I had a moment of profound clarity that changed the course of my life.

Let me explain.

Like many '90s kids, I grew up aware of an iconic scene from the movie *Clueless*—Cher Horowitz staring at her closet before walking up to her computer, which magically assembles outfits from the clothes she owns. It was a fantasy of effortless style, a glimpse into the future of fashion.

At the time, this futuristic magic felt completely out of reach. Sure, we could put a man on the moon, but when would we ever get the technology Cher had in her digital closet? It seemed impossible, but something from this fantasy clearly stuck with me. When I finally watched the entire movie years later, I realized how much that scene had shaped my expectations of getting dressed. Today, I have built and now own the company that transformed that bit of movie-making magic into a real-life smart closet and daily outfit app called Cladwell.

I spent most of my life believing the secret to great style was shopping. I filled my wardrobe, piece by piece, each purchase fueled by the hope of looking "put together." I became the go-to friend for fashion advice and the

PREFACE

authority on what was "in" or "out." I was the last person you'd expect to throw it all away. But then, overwhelmed and underwhelmed at the same time, I did.

Literally.

When I first joined Cladwell, they were already teaching people how to create what they called a capsule wardrobe, convinced that this approach could change lives. Cladwell has always been rooted in helping people love their wardrobes more by owning less.

I wanted to work in fashion, but having a smaller wardrobe wasn't what I had in mind. If anything, I'd thought my work would help justify my retail therapy. Truth be told, I was reluctant to change.

I used to think "capsules" were for those satisfied with wearing neutrals or whose bras were neatly folded—not for someone who loved shopping and a messy drawer as much as I did. But I couldn't, in good conscience, promote capsule wardrobes without experiencing one myself. I was following an unwritten rule I had unknowingly set after earning my degree in marketing, akin to a doctor's creed, but with less dire consequences.

It wasn't until one Saturday eight years ago that I begrudgingly carved out some time to address my overflowing closet. I pulled out every single item of clothing I owned—button ups hanging neatly on wooden hangers, jeans folded in my drawers, T-shirts shoved in the bottom of my woven baskets, and the cocktail dresses I hadn't worn in years hidden in the guest bedroom closet. A project I thought would last an hour or two went well beyond the better half of a day. There was no escaping my past, the good choices and the bad—the hodgepodge of patterns and the clothes with tags still on them sprawled across my ivory-quilted comforter. With little room left on my bed, a huge pile of shoes had spilled onto the carpeted floor next to it.

It looked like a tornado had swept through the aisles of H&M, Old Navy, and Target and terrorized the second story of my house. Staring into the pile of clothes, I couldn't help but wonder, "How did I end up here?"

Today, the answer seems obvious: Before Cladwell came into existence, I believed one thing to be true—a bigger closet was always better. If hours of HGTV had taught me anything, it was that. I loved clothes more than the average girl—definitely more. Shopping wasn't just something I did. It was a hobby I genuinely enjoyed.

My clothes were supposed to be fun, yet the piles of styles on my bed made it painfully obvious that I didn't know who "I" was. Instead of fun fashion choices, I saw all the roles I'd tried to fit into and everyone else's styles I'd taken on as my own. It hit me hard—I wasn't just staring

PREFACE

down a pile of clothes. I was having a full-on identity crisis: Was I the former athlete who wore her oversized North Face sweatpants, and furry, albeit comfortable, Uggs? Was I the recent graduate attempting to pass as a young professional with a skintight black pencil skirt? Or the girl next door who couldn't resist a black-and-white striped T-shirt? Each item whispered stories from different chapters of my life, roles I'd hoped I'd one day fit into, and others I'd completely outgrown.

Yet, for so long, I'd thought fashion *was* my identity. Years ago, I started a little fashion blog, fiddling my way around WordPress during the early days of Web 2.0, when Facebook was taking off and Instagram hadn't yet hit the scene. I turned my fashion blog into a business that secured partnerships with brands I admired like Microsoft and T.J. Maxx. On the side, I wrote the occasional blog article for *The Huffington Post*, attended New York Fashion Week, and even made an appearance on a reality TV show.

At twenty-two, I was diving into what we'd now call being an "influencer," before we had a name for them. Social media was on the rise and tech entrepreneurship was taking off, changing the way we connected, created, and lived our everyday lives. Brands like T.J. Maxx and ShoeDazzle sent me free clothes and gift cards in exchange for my unfettered opinion. I collected and collected, never once considering the impact adding to my wardrobe had on me or the people who made the clothes.

Imagine my surprise when I finally had the chance to work in fashion. Cladwell was my dream employer—a fashion tech startup in the Midwest with a meaningful mission, ready to take on the fast-fashion trend. Just as fast-food chains rely on cheap labor for quick service, the retail industry was beginning to do the same.

And now, here I was, feeling like a complete and utter fraud, staring at the enormous pile of clothes in the middle of my room. Around me, open drawers spilled over with scarves and sweaters, accessories sat on my nightstand, and shoes—so many shoes—lined the walls like a miniature department store that had been ransacked. My life looked as cluttered as my closet. This wasn't imposter syndrome. I was the definition of an imposter—a capsule wardrobe cheerleader by day and a closet hoarder by night.

I really did love capsule wardrobes, though—well, at least the idea of them. But whenever I thought about what it would take to do a closet cleanout, I'd remember the clothes stuffed in my drawers and channel my anxious energy into helping someone else tackle theirs. How long would it be before my coworkers realized that the problem they were so eager to fix was actually mine? Weeks went by, and I continued to keep my secret under wraps.

PREFACE

The idea of a capsule wardrobe wasn't groundbreaking. The French had been doing it for ages; even so, it was a fairly new concept for Americans, who had cultivated a serious shopping habit. Growing up, I assumed if I didn't like my wardrobe, it was because I didn't have the right items. Getting more bang for my buck was my answer, and if that came with bragging rights for how cheaply I bought a new item, that was a huge win in the Midwest.

So of course I had a closet full of clothes. And yet I found myself most mornings staring aimlessly into the abyss, muttering the same five words, "I have nothing to wear." The math wasn't mathing. I'd go shopping to try to find the right piece, only to face the same problem again months later. It was easier to look for a new dress than to deal with the five hanging up that I didn't love.

I was agitated, and I couldn't help but notice how much calmer and self-assured my coworkers seemed. Maybe this capsule wardrobe thing was worth taking seriously in my own life. The tipping point came when I decided I couldn't, in good conscience, market our new product if I hadn't given it a shot myself. So one fateful Saturday morning, a few days before we released our first version to the public, I pulled up our company's newly built website and closely studied the step-by-step guide on how to create a capsule wardrobe. And I decided it was time to give it the old college try.

Sifting through my belongings, one at a time, I held up each piece, detailing what I loved and didn't.

A striped button-up dress, its price tag still dangling, untouched.

A jacket gifted but never worn, yet carrying the weight of guilt.

Wide leg jeans, too snug, held on to with the hope they'd one day fit.

Ballet flats were worn a single time because they gave me blisters.

A sequin tank, shiny and colorful, kept "just in case."

As I sorted them into piles, I tried to understand how each piece had claimed a spot in my life. Some were easy to part with—impulse buys, trends that never quite worked, things I kept out of guilt. Others made me hesitate, reminding me of who I once was or who I thought I should be, scared I might need them again one day. But in the end, I filled eight oversized black trash bags. What was left revealed parts of who I was—pieces that I was unwilling to part ways with and others I'd collected for reasons I didn't fully understand.

Only then could I see the truth—the problem wasn't that I didn't have enough of the right clothes. It was that I couldn't see the ones I loved. Buried beneath the clutter, I found pieces that felt like an extension of the best of me—a perfectly worn-in grey sweater, a loosely fitted, earth-tone button up, a T-shirt dress I'd only worn once, and my go-to boots that always saved the day when nothing else worked. These weren't only the things I reached for out of habit. They were the pieces I loved but had lost in the chaos.

Never in my wildest dreams did I think creating a capsule wardrobe would change the way I live. Yet, in a matter of hours, I began decluttering what had been years in the making. Coming to terms with what I loved meant donating all my trendy heels and accepting that I only ever wore flats. By the end of the cleanout, the items left revealed a version of myself that felt familiar. For once, there was relief that lasted longer than an impulse buy in the aisles of Target.

I felt like I had been sleepwalking through life and was suddenly shaken awake from the dream that "more is better" that I'd subscribed to for so long. I looked around at the room full of stuff and wondered, "How did I end up here?" And where else, other than my style, had I been misled?

That big question, "How did I end up here?," pushed me to confront all the stories I was telling myself without even realizing it. I could now see that I had been running on this hamster wheel, wanting more stuff, more to do, and more goals to hit. I didn't even know who I was anymore.

Clearing the clutter didn't just tidy up my closet. It cleared my mind, making space for me to think for myself.

If you're skeptical that cleaning the closet can have this kind of impact on the average person's life, I completely understand. If the term "minimalism" feels foreign or you've no interest in mastering the art of "tidying up," you're in good company. I grew up in the middle of America, where I didn't have too much, nor too little. My career isn't jam-packed with jet-setting travel that takes me from city to city. My life is far from extravagant. I have a career, a home, and a family. I juggle a life filled with school drop-offs and dinner plans, the constant background noise of group text messages (help us all), a much-needed coffee at 2:00 p.m., and perhaps too much time spent scrolling Instagram. There are deadlines to meet, laundry that never ends, dishes to put away, sports schedules that demand a dedicated calendar, and the occasional quiet moment when I stay in the bathroom longer than is required before heading back out.

It's a full life—maybe not glamorous, but it's mine. And by owning it, I've found the allure of chasing the next big thing has lost its appeal. What I'm after these days is staying grounded, sturdy, down to earth, as they say in the Midwest. I can't help but think there are others out there, just like me, who have craved a calmer way to live—quieter, yet somehow more real and alive.

Whenever life gets messy, I return to the process that led me to my capsule wardrobe. It serves as a road map, guiding me through the noise and helping me focus on what's essential. It has challenged my assumptions about who I thought I was supposed to be—as a woman, an athlete, and an entrepreneur. Each step in the process helps me live a life that feels like mine, not simply a carbon copy of someone else's. It brings me back to myself and grounds me.

Of course, parsing out the old stories and mantras in my life has been more complex than tossing out a high school T-shirt. I needed to lay my thoughts out in front of me, as I had done with my closet.

This book became that space. It wasn't that I lacked words, but I had too many to understand where I stood or what I truly believed. The task of decluttering is ongoing. I'm not sure it will ever be complete, yet each step brings me closer to clarity.

Editing my closet was just the beginning.

INTRODUCTION

The Stories We Carry

If listening to influencers and so-called experts had led to a closet filled with things I didn't love, I had to wonder—what other stories had I been pulled into? Had I forgotten how to create my own? Stories are powerful. Their pull is strong. They tell us what to do—we might not be aware of why we choose to drive a Jeep over a Tesla or go to college over staying in the family business, but chances are, there's a story behind each decision. Even more profoundly, stories tell us who we are.

Let's take the "how to achieve the American Dream" story as an example. It's a story most of us have probably never spoken out loud but could recite if prompted. It goes something like this...

Go to school, get good grades, and aim for excellence by making the honor roll. Participate in extracurricular activities, attend prom, take the SAT or ACT, and get into a good college. Start your career. Work your way up the ladder. Settle down, get married, and have approximately 2.5 kids. Move to a nice neighborhood and live in a big house, complete with an even bigger closet, surrounded by a white picket fence. Prioritize your kids (and their athletics), career, and vacations all while saving in your 401(k). Retire. Travel. Die having lived a happy life.

This is the story most of us grew up with—a story that started so early in life we barely even noticed. Along the way, each milestone acts as a checkpoint, a way to measure if we're keeping up with the "good life" that's been laid out before us, if we've become who we should be.

What happens when we question the story of who we "should" be and insist on being who we really are, living the way we really need to live? It can be disruptive. Take the 2020 Olympics, for example, when Simone Biles, arguably the GOAT (greatest gymnast of all time), withdrew from the Olympics citing the "twisties"—a condition causing gymnasts to lose control in midair, often due to mental stress. The critics were loud, and the message was clear:

She should stick to the script, or face harsh criticism. The reaction was overwhelming and nearly broke the internet: "She can't do that!" they said. And, "Whatever happened to the saying 'no pain, no gain'?" Not to mention "leave it all on the field," and the ever-popular "pain is temporary and glory is forever"?

That was the familiar narrative, and those were the "rules" we all accepted, until this gymnast prioritized her own well-being over the expectations of what an Olympian should do and be. Her decision to withdraw set a precedent and sparked a cultural debate by challenging the story in our heads about what it means to be tough.

Instead of pushing through and possibly getting hurt worse by following the default narrative, Biles made the brave move to step back. And with that step, she made us think about where our culture's beliefs end and ours begin. For everyone watching—especially young girls—Simone Biles's return was more than a comeback. It was proof of a story we're not told nearly enough—the one about choosing yourself and rewriting the narrative on your own terms. A story we can live with, despite what others—or the critics—might think.

From the time we're little, we start crafting stories in an attempt to figure out the world. What we hear or watch play out sticks with us, shaping who we think we should be. As we get older, we often forget to check if those stories we formed some time ago still match up with how we want to live now.

When I started checking on those stories, it was like flipping on a light switch. I saw how much I'd bought into the idea that more is always better—and not just in my closet, but in every aspect of my life. This belief pushed me to work harder, achieve more, and work endlessly to earn approval. Looking back, I can see how it was all too easy to flow with the current, chasing the same milestones everyone else seemed to want—success, money, and respect. Why question a path that promises everything we're told to value, everything we're assured will lead to wild success? My focus, understandably, was on fitting in, striving to belong.

For the past two years, I've written and rewritten the essays that make up this book, piecing them together like a puzzle. I've spent days on my living room floor, shuffling pages, rearranging experiences, and searching for the order that makes it all make sense. Reading this book is like opening the doors to my mind, with pages of stories sprawled out, spilling onto the carpeted floor. I'm picking each one up, holding it to the light, and asking myself: What do I love? What have I outgrown? It's an invitation to listen in as I sort through it all.

INTRODUCTION

Will it be messy? It will. That's because I'm going to tell you my story in the same way I started uncovering it myself: by peeling back each layer as it came to light and figuring out where it belonged, what lesson it was teaching me. That's why the following pages don't flow in chronological order—they flow in the order of lessons learned.

Here's what I know: Life isn't about having everything perfectly in place. It's about discovering—or in some cases, remembering—what makes us come to life—creating, connecting, setting our own pace, and realizing that beauty and love are so much bigger than what we can buy.

It's in the messiness that I've found where the real story begins.

PART ONE

Culture

What We Never Thought to Question

"

We seldom realize, for example, that our most private thoughts and emotions are not actually our own. For we think in terms of languages and images which we did not invent, but which were given to us by our society.

"

— ALAN WATTS

Small Town, *Big* World

TWO YOUNG FISH WERE SWIMMING ALONG WHEN they ran into an older fish who asked, "Morning, boys, how's the water?" The young fish swam on, puzzled, and after a while, one turned to the other and asked, "What the hell is water?"

Like those fish, I couldn't see the culture I was swimming in. Growing up in a place where everyone knew my name, I didn't question the unspoken rules or expectations. I absorbed them. I thought the way things were was simply the way life was meant to be lived.

That was life in Morristown, Indiana.

It was quiet. Nestled between the vast cornfields and the soft hum of cicadas, there's a way of life that doesn't beg for attention. I was one of a thousand people in a small town miles outside Indianapolis, in the heart of the heartland. Without a single stoplight, there was no reason to slow down and observe this way of life.

It was simple. The Midwest has an unpretentious charm. Free from the glitz of New York City or the cool vibe of California, it's understated. In my twenties, I wanted to live elsewhere, thinking new horizons held the key to a more exciting life. As I jumped from place to place, I've come to appreciate the simplicity the so-called flyover country offers.

It was familiar. The town was filled with my family, literally. My grandparents, parents, aunts, and uncles all went to the same school, a stone's throw away from my childhood home. We all lived within five minutes of each other. Directions weren't necessary, but if we had to give them to others, it was by landmarks and people, not by street names.

"Turn left before the Nolans' house, then right after you pass the white barn and silos. You'll see my brother's place across from the Everharts' farm."

I lived across from the school on the stretch of Highway 52, where a little green sign signifies a new small town every few miles. Our house sat less than a few blocks from the train tracks and half a mile from the grain bins that purred in the fall. My home was like a revolving door with a lock that didn't work for nearly thirteen years. We'd sit on the front porch glider, chatting with the same set of neighbors complaining that the traffic was getting louder.

There were a few staple "characters" in town. We knew our town marshal by one name only, Henry. For one season, he doubled as a substitute teacher at my high school, formerly his. The town drunk was another. We would see him riding his moped after losing his license, no one questioning the legality of that. Then there was Mower Boy—a kid who chose a lawn mower as his means of transportation through the alleyways. On the main stretch of Highway 52 sit a few family-owned restaurants. One is where guests as famous as past presidents and Indiana native Jane Pauley, a former *Today Show* anchor, once dined. The other is where the older men, including my dad, gathered at "the round table" in the morning to have coffee and do their form of gossiping.

Traditions mattered in Morristown. Basketball, even more so. After a big win in the County or Sectional tournament, the athletes would climb on top of a fire truck, where they sat with feet dangling over the side of it as they took a victory lap. Everyone in town would come out onto their front porch, cheering them on as they made their loop around town. Last but not least, there was the annual Derby Days Fish Fry that marked the end of summer. The parade would take place directly in front of my house. Class reunion floats, bands, tractors, and every fire truck imaginable would follow each other. Behind them were boys walking their soapbox derby cars, gearing up for the race down the one hill in town.

Like any tight-knit community, our town thrived on a strong rumor mill. People also knew how to rally together, whether behind a team of girls heading for their school's first state title or a boy who unexpectedly found out he had cancer. Everyone had a role, from the cake lady to the bank teller; we were farmers, small business owners, and factory workers. The few who held the wealth used it to discreetly influence politics in town. This place came with a history where everyone really did know your name. We knew them all.

Living in a place means culture isn't something you see—it's something you live every day. It's woven into dinner table conversations, game nights, and traditions passed down through generations. Some of those simple-seeming traditions carry big ideas—look closely, and you'll see the subtle cues about what status matters, who holds influence, and how power plays out. They shaped the way I saw the world.

Early on, I learned that as a Hoosier, being an athlete earned me respect and a sense of belonging—just like wearing low-rise jeans did among my friends. These weren't trends I followed. They were ways to fit in.

What I didn't realize was that I wasn't living in Mayberry. There were no commercial breaks, no perfect TV endings—just a complicated mix of cultural messages influencing my daily life in ways I didn't fully understand at the time.

When life feels overwhelming, it's human instinct to look outside ourselves for answers—to the people around us, the places we've known, the voices telling us how to live. For me, that often meant scrolling Instagram for advice or clinging to outdated ideas of success. Lately, I've started to wonder: How long have I been looking for a different way to live in places that held answers for others yet never fit me?

For a long time, I didn't think about how these cultural norms shaped my sense of self. At all. I lived in a small town that valued sports and tradition, and I never questioned whether those things aligned with who I was at my core. They simply were. I absorbed them, much like I breathed the air around me. But as I got older, I started to wonder: Was I shaping my life, or was it being shaped for me?

The stories I've been holding on to—about success, fashion, and who I'm supposed to be—are ones I picked up along the way without even noticing. Why did I hold on to these ideas? Was it for comfort, out of fear, or simply because it's what everyone else did? Now, as I sift through these stories and old assumptions, I'm uncovering parts of the past that explain so much about the present. It's like finding an old shirt in the back of my closet and wondering why I ever kept it. These days, I find myself with more questions than answers.

Maybe that's okay.

Measuring *Up*

ELEMENTARY SCHOOL WAS THE FIRST TIME I BEcame aware of the space I took up in the world. I was often praised for my height. "You're taller than most of the boys," they'd say. I'd notice the surprise in their voices, as if my personal growth were an accomplishment, but I had no more control of my height than I did my frizzy hair. I suppose standing out from my classmates could have easily made me self-conscious, though it had the opposite effect. Living in a place that valued athletics, being tall was an advantage. I'd stand next to the boys closest to me, always measuring myself against them, a kind of foretelling that wouldn't show up until much later in life.

The smack talk about whether or not I could beat the boys started in second grade. I skipped hanging on the monkey bars for an opportunity to resolve the debate out on the blacktop pavement at recess: challenging each boy to a game of one-on-one. At first, it felt fun—a way to stand out and fit in at the same time. But over time, I began to feel the weight of that identity. If being a good athlete gave me status, what would happen if I stopped measuring up? The praise I received for my height and talent started to feel less like a compliment and more like a treadmill I had hopped on with an expectation I had to keep running after. Being a good athlete became such a big part of my identity that it terrified me to think what would happen if I wasn't one.

What would others think of me? Worse, if they disapproved, what would I think about myself? I took others' opinions very seriously and believed that with enough hard work, I could impress them all. And if I couldn't do it myself—ironically, I was fully aware of how little control I had over my own body and my own life—I was prepared to give the things beyond my control to a higher power. Every night, I prayed to be tall.

Mr. Carmichael, who coached the high school boys' basketball team and taught my elementary PE class, noticed my drive early on. He *believed* in Indiana basketball and took it upon himself to ensure that it was integrated into our school's curriculum, for our indoctrination. Without fail, on a day when he'd have to substitute for the music teacher, he'd roll in the TV on a cart, swapping our music recorders for a screening of the film *Hoosiers*. It wasn't surprising that this was his movie of choice—the real-life coach was a Morristown High School alum and our elementary principal made a guest appearance in the film as a referee. You couldn't make this up—the depths of Hoosier Hysteria were honestly limitless.

I respected Mr. Carmichael. He was the first person I had met outside my family who valued basketball as much as we did. He'd tell me tales about how Larry Bird would get up early to get shots in before school. I begged my mom for a giant poster board from Walmart so I could draw lines across it, crafting a rudimentary chart resembling an Excel spreadsheet. Each box represented a tiny commitment I could measure, proof I was trying hard.

That year, I woke up early before school began, shooting outside next to a sign that hung in my driveway just above the garage door: "Miss Basketball 2005." Bear in mind, it was 1998. After shooting a hundred shots, I'd rush inside to grab a black permanent marker, adding a check to the box on the chart before heading off to school.

It's hard to pinpoint exactly what caught Mr. Carmichael's attention—maybe he noticed I was tall. Maybe it was my love for the game. Or my family's coaching history. Regardless of the reason, Mr. Carmichael gave me my first real taste of competition in the fourth grade. He introduced me to "The Elks Club Hoop Shoot" when I was ten years old. The organization finally let girls participate in 1974. The winner from our school would get to move on to compete against the best in the county. I'd go on to win in my age bracket every year, moving to the next round.

By the time fourth grade rolled around, my best friend Allie and I were hand-selected to play AAU. Previous stints of playing in recreational leagues paled in comparison. This felt different, as if we had earned our spot in school as top athletes. The roster was filled with girls from other schools. Our uniforms had fancy material featuring teal and purple team colors, last names on the back of our jerseys, and numbers we got to choose. This was a gateway to a broader universe—players, coaches, and parents who cared about sports as much as I did, showing up to play four or five games on the weekends.

As we went to more tournaments, one particular team stood out; the girls wore shiny red and black uniforms and a matching warm-up set, and the coach wasn't a dad. I watched Katie Gearlds play on Indiana's Finest

Black Cats, a fifteen-and-under AAU basketball team. She was a future Indiana Miss Basketball, an All-American at Purdue with a professional stint in the WNBA. She eventually circled back to become the head coach for Purdue University's women's team. She was the best player I had seen since April McDivitt, another Indiana Miss Basketball who went on to play under the legendary Pat Summitt at the University of Tennessee. These were my role models, and the moment I saw Katie play, a new marker was set.

That year, through several tryouts, I earned a spot on Indiana's Finest Black Cats. Unlike many teammates from Indianapolis, I came from a small town. Working hard had gotten me to the highest levels of Indiana basketball at the ripe old age of eleven. And it reinforced everything I wanted to believe about how the world worked.

We traveled around the Midwest, staying in hotels and playing in hot summer gyms without air-conditioning. Playing at the highest levels looked different than I had imagined. My dad was not like the other girls' dads. He never played or obsessed over watching sports. Instead, he was a dreamer and a quiet supporter who saw this experience as an opportunity for me to fuel my own dreams. Never once did he yell or criticize me. Never did he lecture about what I could have done better after the games.

One weekend, the stark contrast in parenting styles was evident when a teammate's dad had to fill in as a coach. The game intensified as the girls on the other team gained the upper hand, and he called for a time-out. We sat on the bench. He squatted down, a tiny bald man, but you wouldn't know it by the way he screamed. I thought the teal-blue vein running down the left side of his face would pop out of his forehead. In a fit of anger directed at his daughter, he took off his glasses, throwing them with such force they shattered upon hitting the ground. Even as a young kid, I remember thinking he was completely unhinged. I expected the intensity of drills and practices but was unprepared for the dads or the undercurrent of politics that determined our playing time. They weren't just involved. They were entrenched, creating a pressure-cooker environment, including the critical analysis that followed each game. It seemed everyone had an opinion of how we performed, and they all sat in the stands. Though we were only eleven at the time, each girl on that team eventually became part of the 7 percent of high school athletes who went on to play sports in college, including producing Indiana's Miss Basketball my senior year.

As my skills improved over time, a coach from a larger nearby school noticed me during eighth grade. His attention was flattering, albeit bordering on recruiting, which was not legal then. At every run-in, he would ask the same question: "Do you want to be a big fish in a small pond or a small fish in a big pond?"

Staying at my small school, I was determined to get a scholarship and prove him wrong. I turned his skepticism into motivation, learning to dribble with blinders and even teaching myself to eat with my left hand—a habit that I still have today. My singular focus was on improving and becoming tougher to guard on the court.

I'm not telling you this to shed light on my AAU seasons or show you how good or not good I was as a kid. I am sharing this to emphasize how early our stories begin. You don't have to be a superstar like Serena Williams or Steph Curry to experience the pressure of performance. You don't even have to be an athlete. Maybe you excelled in academia and focused on making the honor roll. Or you were a star in theater and set your mind on getting the lead role in the play. Whatever your goals were, chances are, like me, you set those goals based on a story you were living well before your brain had fully developed.

And the story was being told by people you respected. Adults who gathered around you, the kid with big ambitions, to help you succeed. Coaches and trainers, largely well-meaning, who pushed you toward the traditional idea of success, rarely stopping to ask what it actually meant to you or how it felt. To be fair, I'm not sure if I could have articulated it even if they had asked me what I wanted.

Don't get me wrong; there were plenty of positives in my years in sports. Sports taught me a lot about life—like how much discipline and dedication it takes to be great, and the kind of grit you need to pick yourself up after a fall. It also showed me the harder side, all the rules and expectations you have to meet. Growing up in a town where sports were a big deal, being good at them gave me a sort of celebrity status, setting me apart and bringing privileges that others didn't have.

Basketball was my first love. Over time, though, the line between what I loved and what was expected of me began to blur. I endured playing through blistered feet and leg cramps, and I even battled mono—twice, much to everyone's surprise, including my doctor's. It started to feel like success wasn't possible unless it came with pain.

Hard work has always been at the core of what I believe. It earned me a full scholarship to college, but at some point, it became more than a value. It became a weight. I started tying my self-worth to what I achieved, convinced that the next milestone would finally bring relief. Yet every success only raised the bar, pushing me toward the next challenge. I was afraid that slowing down would make people think less of me—that I wasn't willing to go the extra mile. These beliefs were so deeply ingrained that I never stopped to consider another way to live—one that didn't have to feel so hard or stressful.

Where hustling or busyness weren't prerequisites.

Not Enough *Room*

HIGH SCHOOL WAS A BREEDING GROUND FOR competition, especially among the girls. I might have been the biggest tomboy in my friend group, but we were all equally athletic. These were the same girls who, back in elementary school, would team up with me to challenge the boys. We prized winning over how we looked.

Our grade was known for being the good girls, the ones who followed the rules and did what was expected. We spent our summers riding bikes, celebrating birthdays in each other's backyards, and dedicating hours in the gym at sports camps. By the time high school came around, I felt a deep sense of comfort with my friends. I never worried about where I fit in. The older we got, the more attention we started getting from some of the boys. It came not despite our athletic ability but because of it. In small-town Indiana, being a good athlete was attractive. We weren't cheerleaders dating the quarterbacks. We were athletes dating athletes. It never even crossed my mind to downplay my ability. I think the guys I dated liked the challenge of knowing I could easily outshoot them in a game of PIG.

My best friend Allie was no different. We had been at each other's side since we were five or so. I don't remember how our friendship started, but I remember how it all ended.

A short drive up the hill in town sat her house, a small ranch. A few knocks on the door. A few more to assure her family I wasn't leaving the front porch until we talked. I was there to repair a friendship that, over weeks, had fallen apart without explanation.

There were whispers on the other side when her brother finally let me in. We walked down the narrow hallway to the back of the house, my heart beating faster than I'd ever felt.

The door opened to her parents' bedroom, revealing familiar spaces filled with nostalgia. We sat down. I, on one side of the bed with the puffy, sky-blue comforter. She and her mom were on the other. At the corner of my eye was where we used to play dress-up, our little faces framed by crimped hair as we admired ourselves in a massive mirror that spanned the entire vanity.

Her mom, sitting on the edge of the bed, began recounting a story from spring break in painstaking detail. "I saw you approach him [referring to Allie's ex-fling]. Sticking out your chest." My heart sank to the pit of my stomach.

It sounds so silly to write down, like a bad episode of *Saved by the Bell*. Months earlier, I had gone on spring break with Allie's family. Spring break was less of an escape than a change of scenery. The same town and familiar faces relocated miles away with an ocean backdrop. She had previously had a short fling with a boy she met from a neighboring town, only to end it a month later. Fresh out of a two-year relationship myself, I wasn't on the lookout for another fleeting high school romance. I was set on enjoying this vacation carefree with no attachments.

At a loss for words, I couldn't muster a defense or even clear the air. Growing up, discussions about our bodies were nonexistent. Not only had I never consciously stuck out my chest, but I barely acknowledged I had one. The only time it came up was when I needed to pack a clean sports bra. I wanted my friend back and this, whatever this was, to go away.

Her mom's story had a logic to it. From her side, a girl has feelings for a boy, ends the relationship, and expects her friends to steer clear. I'd watched enough of the Zack Morris, A.C. Slater, and Kelly Kapowski love triangle to understand the unspoken rule: You don't let your feelings interfere with friendships. I took a deep breath, ready to apologize for what I thought was a simple misunderstanding. I hoped that, once and for all, we could clear the air and return to regularly scheduled programming, but nothing I said seemed to matter. Nor was it believed. Her mother was judge, jury, and friendship-executioner. I had betrayed her daughter's trust and "she'd always expected this to happen." (Dagger to the heart.)

In that moment, I realized something that took years to fully understand: Some conflicts can't be solved with a simple apology. I had grown up believing that if you said sorry, things would be made right again. We're taught this over and over again when we tell kids to say sorry after not sharing a toy. But this was different. My words didn't carry the power to fix what had already been decided about me. With adrenaline pumping through every ounce of my body, I attempted to dodge the punches, with each stinging a little more as they flew out of her mom's mouth.

I'll never know what my friend thought. She didn't speak up, but there was no mistaking where her mother stood. I kept wondering how an encounter I barely recalled could be so misconstrued. I had one attempt to make things right, so I sat up tall on the bed, my palms slick with sweat as my heart pounded harder than I had ever thought possible. Drawing on every bit of courage, I spoke the only words I could find. "I'm so sorry."

I thought an apology could glue it back together. I stood up, heart heavy, knowing deep down it was the last time I'd step foot in her house. Thoughts filled my mind as I passed the spot where we choreographed dances to the Backstreet Boys, played Super Mario Brothers on the Nintendo 64, and even shaved our legs for the first time. I couldn't understand how a simple misunderstanding could erase all of that. Or why my apology did not make things right.

Looking back, I can see how the simple stories we're told as kids about friendship and fixing conflicts—like saying sorry to make everything better—don't always hold up as we grow older. Life gets more complicated. I remember asking for forgiveness that day, hoping her mom would let it go, but it never came.

Worse, I was shunned, like an Amish person being disciplined for violating certain principles. Anytime I came near Allie or one of her family members, they shut me out like I imagined the Amish would. I would walk in. They would walk out. I would say something. They would pretend like I didn't. It was an art, not a science. My entire family, including a few loyal friends, were all ostracized by association.

At school, our situation was largely hidden. However, in a class with less than twenty-five girls, I would see disbelief on the faces of others when I'd inevitably have to explain why we no longer talked.

It sounds so melodramatic now as I sit here and type. Why would an entire family who had been our friends for two generations disown mine, especially given it centered around a high school boy?

But it was my reality for two years, playing out every day like a bad teen movie. Picture me grabbing my lunch as usual and heading to my seat, where Allie and the other girls ignored me. It happened every day, until I reached the breaking point. Once again, faced with the silent treatment from the girls whispering on the other end of the lunch table, anger flooded me. My palms were sweaty, and my heart raced, but I couldn't contain it this time. On impulse, I stood up, and words spilled out: "I can hear you talking. If you won't speak to me, then I'm leaving. Who's coming with me?"

I had inadvertently planted my stake in the ground. I took a deep breath, lifted my plastic lunch tray, and walked out, unaware if anyone was following or not. As I stood in the hallway, fury and shock flooded over me. I was shaking, surprised by the sudden ability to find my voice. Where had it been all this time?

See, the thing is, when our friends began choosing sides, I knew, without a doubt, whose side they would take. Allie always had a natural charm, effortlessly taking on the role of the popular girl among our friends. She was the first to get her ears pierced, wore the best clothes, and had shiny, long hair and flawless skin. They would go with her, and I understood that.

Something about no longer pretending had made the ground shift beneath me. I realized this wasn't about making things right with my friend—it was the start of understanding that staying quiet just to keep the peace wasn't the answer. Letting go of that old story, like tossing out a pair of shorts that no longer fit, brought me closer to who I really was.

I used to believe in the adage that time heals all wounds. However, the last two years of high school were a special slice of hell that made me question who I was. I'll never know for sure what or where it all went wrong, but I have learned this: Each season of our lives has the potential to change us, to loosen the grip of what once defined who we were, but only if we stay open.

Only if we let it.

Great Expectations

STANDING UP FOR MYSELF IN THE HIGH SCHOOL lunchroom wasn't just about that one moment. It was about unlearning a story I'd carried with me for years—the idea that keeping the peace was more important than speaking the truth.

Imagine me, sitting outside my new classroom, waiting for my pre-kindergarten assessment. It was my first real academic test. As a five-year-old, I didn't have any preconceived notions or expectations. When the teacher asked me questions, I was to answer them the best I could.

To start things off, she turned to me and asked, "Can you tell me what a sail is?"

I sat up tall in my orange plastic chair and spoke with the conviction only a five-year-old could deliver. Confidently, I stated, "A sale is when you go to a garage and buy something. A garage sale."

My teacher couldn't help but laugh. Looking back, how could she not? An innocent five-year-old describing the concept of a bargain to a grown woman. But with each laugh, I became increasingly self-aware. I began to crumble from the inside out, unsure how to stop the spiral. It was the first time I really doubted myself. And the rejection was loud. (In my defense, a sale is far more common than a sail in the middle of rural Indiana. I stand by my answer.)

In my mind, that day marked my first failure to meet someone else's expectations. At five years old, I added a new narrative to my collection: It was no longer safe to speak my mind without first trying to guess what was on someone else's.

Thus began a lifelong habit of holding back when I wanted to say something, because I might be wrong. And only speaking up when I was sure it was exactly what others wanted to hear. To keep everyone happy, I ended up building walls around myself, opting for what felt safe to protect me from the pressures of the outside world. I didn't realize that every time I did this, I was making it harder to stand on solid ground. I thought that if I worked hard, followed all the rules in school, did well in sports, and checked off the next milestone, I'd be set up for success.

But the blueprint I was following wasn't leading where I thought it would. I remember crossing the street and biking up the only hill in town to Mamaw and Papaw's. I'd let myself into the back of the house where the kitchen and dining room melded together and plates hung as decor, bordering the walls. Mamaw and I were two peas in a pod, yet every visit began with Papaw, seated in his rocking chair at the center of the wooden dining room table, the air tinged with the familiar scent of cinnamon Dentyne gum.

Papaw was a legend. He was a business teacher and made his mark as the head coach of the boys' and girls' basketball teams. Back when towns the size of ours rarely had a chance against the bigger schools, he garnered respect by clinching multiple titles. He coached at the same time as John Wooden and Marvin Wood—also legends who, as players themselves, experienced Hoosier Hysteria. Wooden grew up sixty miles west of where I lived. Like us, he, too, was surrounded by farmland. He was a player of the game who became known later in life for climbing the ranks as one of the most successful college coaches in history, leading

UCLA to ten NCAA titles in twelve seasons with players like Kareem Abdul-Jabbar and Bill Walton, who went on to have successful NBA careers. Seven of these were an unprecedented series of back-to-back victories.

Then there was Marvin Wood, known in Morristown as an alum but everywhere else as the famous coach of the 1954 Indiana Basketball State Championship team from Milan High School. Milan, also surrounded by fields, was sixty miles east of my hometown. Their team was the classic underdog in a David versus Goliath story that inspired the iconic movie *Hoosiers*.

Each coach defined the Hoosier mentality long before Bobby Knight's hotheaded approach came along. They were successful and known for their quiet confidence, never raising their voice too loud while commanding the respect of their players. They imparted life lessons on the basics: hard work, humility, character, and preparation. They measured success by something other than what was shown on the scoreboard.

All of this came down to me through my mother, who was cut from the same cloth as Papaw. She, too, was a coach who walked through life with a calm, steady exterior—a leader with unmistakable clarity, discerning right from wrong. More than anything, she was a poster child for responsibility, always holding herself to the highest standard.

GREAT EXPECTATIONS

Mom, or Rosie, as most affectionately call her, has a timeless quality. In many ways, she was meant for another era. She would have thrived among the pages of a Jane Austen novel, where manners, societal structures, and social etiquette were paramount. Yet, had fate shifted her birth by a mere decade, I can imagine her riding the wave of the modern woman, completing her college education, a path she still recalls with a tinge of regret for not finishing—and, like her dad, stepping into the role of an athletic director.

My mom is not one to sit back or sit down. She has an innate ability to organize and manage multiple things at once. Need to schedule a family birthday party? Rosie's your go-to. Did someone have an emergency? Rosie's already cooking a homemade meal. I've never seen someone always on the move as much as she is.

At a time when individualism is celebrated, my mom prioritizes gatherings. She is proper and a stickler for rules, not in a snobbish way where your fork and knife have to be positioned in their proper places, but in making sure everyone is taken care of at all times. In every social situation, she knows what to do. To this day, I can't bring myself to wear jeans to a baby shower because it feels too casual. Nor can I host a party without having more than enough food.

Although she had a traditional gender role as a stay-at-home mom, taking care of the house and kids—she was a rule follower, for the most part—a different story emerged beneath the surface. Psychologists say we learn more from observing the actions of those around us than from their words. I couldn't agree more. What I saw was a woman who was the epitome of a matriarch, setting the table and also running the show. I watched her direct her sisters and family at large like a CEO directs a team full of employees.

I also saw the moments when she broke free of expectations. For instance, she refused to cook on Sundays. Sundays were marked by a long day at church, followed by the smell of pizza in the evenings. She would pull the leaves out from underneath the wooden table, extending it to full size so the extended family could gather around. When the family came over, we got the good stuff, thin-crust Pizza Hut, rather than frozen out of the box.

We occasionally reserved Sunday evenings for a game of basketball out on our concrete driveway, which was etched with cracks and a slight slant before it met the road that made dribbling a challenge in and of itself. Aunts who previously played basketball, and uncles who chose to play in jeans and work boots. All this occurred under the Sunday night lights my dad had hung at the top of the telephone pole so I could shoot past dark. Being from Indiana, basketball ran through my blood. I was a certified gym rat, tagging along to practice with my mom as she coached. It was a love language steeped in tradition for our state, town, and family.

The women in my family were the ones who cared more about sports, defying cultural expectations in many ways—always coaching, playing, rooting for the IU basketball team, and never missing a Peyton Manning football game. My mom even became a referee for a season of life, a move I wouldn't dare make. Sports weren't a hobby. They were an essential part of my life.

No one explicitly said I needed to excel in sports or follow the rules like a good girl, but my identity was deeply molded by what I saw happening around me. Before writing this book, I couldn't have told you which beliefs or values were part of my origin story and which belonged to my family or my hometown. You could say they were cluttered. Entangled to the point it was difficult to know what I believed and what was added over time.

We like to think the paths we choose and the identities we form are entirely our own making. Sometimes, though, that very belief in our independence becomes our greatest blind spot. From the moment we open our eyes, our families, and the very ground we play on, give us our first dose of the water we're swimming in—and we swim until it becomes so familiar we can't even see it. I can't say my upbringing was any different.

Getting to know myself and my family history has been far more complicated than simply tracing a family tree on Ancestry.com. Such a search can't tell me which stories have taken root in my life. For the first time, I'm asking whether my biggest ambitions are what I love, or are they stories I've gathered along the way because everyone else seemed to think they were important?

Female.
Athlete.

BEING GOOD AT BASKETBALL EARNED ME A SILENT kind of respect. It allowed me to cross an invisible boundary and simply be one of the guys, a boundary that traditionally "girls' sports" like volleyball couldn't breach.

There was always this tug-of-war—trying to earn the guys' respect while also wanting to be accepted by the girls. I was constantly balancing a double-edged sword that the boys in my grade never seemed to worry about: needing to be both liked and admired. Both strong and skinny.

And skinny, unlike the other things, could be measured. It started with the annual physical during my freshman year in high school. In the school gym, I held the paper with my results—my personal information—close to me. The thought of anyone discovering whether or not I checked yes next to my last cycle made me cringe.

On the form, it stated my height and weight in black and white: 5 feet 9 inches and 110 pounds. Heading into my freshman year, my body resembled a stick more than an athlete. Unbeknownst to me, this body I had gave me a type of unearned privilege. I was tall enough to grab rebounds in the post and thin enough to fit the conventional female mold.

This was the first time I'd seriously confronted these numbers; sports had acted as a shield against the body image insecurities that many girls begin to face as early as ten or eleven. At the same time, my coaches constantly told me I needed to be bigger and stronger, urging me to hit the weight room and bulk up. And I couldn't avoid overhearing the casual and often cruel remarks made about other girls' bodies. I may have been sipping the poisonous messages more slowly than others, but I was still drinking the arsenic, unaware of it spreading through my bloodstream. I hadn't felt its full effects yet.

Perhaps surprisingly, even by the summer before college, I remained blissfully unconcerned about my weight. I had a fast metabolism, having played three sports, and food was...food. I'd make bagel bites after school and eat orange push-ups whenever my heart desired.

Then one day, during open gym, I ran into Grace. The previous year, she had been named the best basketball player in Shelby County. Even though we attended different schools, we made a point of playing together in the off-season. Her reputation as a player was high, and there was always mutual respect between us. Grace, a year older than me, had a full year of college under her belt. I looked up to her as someone who could shed light on my future.

I was thrown when, a little later that evening, a friend said Grace had gained the dreaded "freshman fifteen." I was aware of the term, but it had meant little to me until now. With college quickly approaching, I leaned in to pay closer attention. All of a sudden I understood that those fifteen pounds were more than just weight. Acquiring them seemingly opened a secret passageway for uninvited opinions and snap judgments.

Grace's athletic ability on the court no longer protected her from a few thoughtless remarks off of it. Now that she was out of her high school glory days and in the real world, it seemed as though something had changed. Grace, to my knowledge, didn't know people were talking. But I did.

Later that fall, I walked into my college classroom and was greeted by a sea of U-shaped desks that filled the entire space, creating a labyrinth-like atmosphere. I quickly made my way to the back corner, hoping to blend in with the background and avoid drawing attention. This class was one of my least favorite, and I preferred to go unnoticed.

Settling in, my friend's voice cut through the noise: "You look great." Flattered, I thanked her and brushed it off as a casual remark, but I knew the only change in my appearance was the fact that I had lost five pounds. The team's intense workout routine was making it harder to keep up the calories. That small, otherwise meaningless comment shifted everything for me.

I honestly had never considered my size a factor in how I looked until that day. The poison had finally made its way to my bones. How could it not? I had been lucky to have made it this far. I don't know what it was about the timing of what she said, but it awoke something within me that had always been there.

Maybe it had such a profound effect because my college coach was on a health journey of his own around the same time. He had always been a runner, though, admittedly, the kind that would exercise to indulge in a box of donuts at the finish line. He struggled with discipline around food, and his coping mechanism was to out-exercise his craving for sweets. That spring, he joined WeightWatchers, and after seeing results, he developed his version of the program for our team to follow during our summer break. He handed out calendar printouts, directing us to document our daily meals, workouts, and weekly weigh-ins. By summer's end, these charts were our tickets back onto the court, tangible proof that we were in good enough shape to play.

Like any rule follower, I didn't want to just meet the bar he set. I wanted to exceed it. I worked out, tracked my endless salads, and ran my first 5K while obsessively filling out every day of the calendar. I was determined not to go over the "perfect" number I had made up in my mind: 123 pounds. Standing on the scale became my daily ritual. Pinching my sides to ensure there was no "extra" skin. Striking a superwoman stance to measure my waist with my hands. My self-worth was contingent on my middle fingers touching in front of the center of my stomach. If I overate, I'd fit in extra workouts. Most days, I'd limit myself to a single ninety-calorie Special K bar while wrestling with guilt when I'd inevitably want another.

It turned out that what worked for a man in his forties wasn't quite right for a woman in her twenties. My coaches, perhaps not fully aware of the struggles I was facing internally, called me into their office. They noticed the detailed tracking and extreme lengths of my training, though they were quick not to ask too many questions about what was going on. I could sense their concern, yet they still praised my self-control and discipline. If there was any doubt about my battling an eating disorder at the start of the summer, there was a chart that undeniably confirmed it by the end.

I craved that sense of protection that Grace had lost one year out of being a high school athlete, and I clung to it as long as I could. Balancing the strength needed to play college athletics while fitting into the classic ideals of white femininity was an impossible feat. But my struggle went largely unaddressed—one of the "perks" of playing at a Division II school that had only one physical therapist for all the sports. That meant the men's teams got most of the attention. If you weren't a star on the women's team, you were pretty much on your own.

During my senior year, it got harder to ignore what was going on. My body started to physically break down. My knee gave way during our first practice, as if it was telling me, "You're done here." But giving up? That wasn't in my psyche. I remember lying there under the basket, taking forever to get up, and then limping off to the trainer's room where all I got was some ice and a quick, "Not much more I can do." That year tested me, physically and mentally.

There was one game in particular that was soul-crushing. It was late in the season with my senior year coming to an end. Our athletic director had set up a game back in Indiana at the historic Hinkle Fieldhouse. It was in the same gym where I had won a volleyball state championship years earlier, but it was unusual for a college game, because I had family in the stands. I rarely got to play in front of friends and family, with my college being eight hours away from home. We always tried extra hard when people we knew were in the crowd, but on this night it didn't help. We played horribly, losing by twenty.

Sitting in the locker room with my back against the cold metal, every fiber of my being was on high alert. Our coach was yelling more than usual, and his anger quickly shifted to shaming. He went off on us, saying we should be embarrassed to even show our faces to our friends and family. I kept my head down, avoiding eye contact, while sweat dripped down the sides of my temples. I was the only one who actually had "friends and family" there. They didn't care if we lost by fifty—they came regardless of the scoreboard.

Every instinct told me to walk out, yet years of conditioning to respect the coach and trust the people in charge kept me seated. So, I bit my tongue that day and thereafter. I spent the rest of my senior year reflecting on how things that appear peaceful on the surface are often about someone choosing not to rock the boat.

There were aspects of playing sports I wouldn't trade. Learning teamwork and how to push myself helped me get to where I am now, but when I graduated, the phrase "There is no 'I' in team" rang truer than ever. I had conformed so much that I barely recognized my voice. Any sense of "I" had been lost. As my athletic career was coming to a close, so were the things that had always defined me. I had earned my degree, but it made me face the reality that the label—"athlete"—would soon fade.

To the world, I was no more than a woman.

Tomboy

WHAT IS A WOMAN, ANYWAY? WHO'S TO SAY? My mamaw went her entire life without pumping her own gas, yet she is the most well-traveled person I know, having journeyed around the world and back. In fourth grade, she introduced me to "day trips."

After joining the Ambassadair Travel Group, a travel club that charged a $99 membership plus a $199 excursion fee that came with airfare, transportation, a meal, and its own Boeing 720 plane, we could jet off anywhere for a day. The catch? These trips were whirlwinds. We'd wake at 3:00 a.m., be at the Indianapolis airport by 4:00 a.m., and depart by 6:00 a.m. By 11:00 p.m. that same night, we'd be back home asleep in our beds.

This was a different day and age, pre-9/11, before airport security had tightened. Back then, the rules were more relaxed. It wasn't uncommon to greet your family or friends at their gate because there was no security to stop you from doing so. The biggest concern when flying might have been whether your luggage would fit in the overhead bin.

On my first trip, I pretended to be Audrey, taking the ticket of my mamaw's friend, who canceled at the last minute. A Betsy Ross impersonator walked around as our in-gate entertainment, and I managed to go into the cockpit to meet the woman piloting our plane before flying to Valley Forge, Pennsylvania. It's jarring sometimes to think about how much has changed.

We flew to California for a day trip. My hair was pulled back in a ponytail, with flyaways peeking above my ears. I wore my tennis shoes, knee-high socks, black mesh shorts, and a long gray Nike Basketball T-shirt, making a point of rolling up the sleeves to wear it more like a tank top.

I had style—just not the type you might imagine. Maybe heading to the land of luxury and Hollywood elites, where Bob Hope vacationed and the rich and famous owned homes, called for an outfit that was...let's say, nicer. But there I was, sporting my well-loved, cozy outfit—the kind that felt right, no matter where I traveled. I don't recall my mom saying anything. She must have known it wouldn't have mattered.

Palm Springs became one of my favorite places. I adored the way the mountains lined the streets, the desert's sandy tones mixed with the palm trees' green hues, and the mid-century houses nestled between them both. The outdoor café misters and distant windmills left me wondering: Why doesn't everyone live here?

As we walked down the street, I spotted a statue of Lucille Ball. I loved staying up late and watching Nick at Nite with my dad. We'd laugh at *I Love Lucy*. Was it her comedic timing? Or the fact she couldn't help but be unabashedly herself no matter how many times Ricky would say, "Lucy!" Either way, it called for a picture—Mamaw on the left, me on the right. Looking at it now, I see exactly who I was—a tomboy through and through, dressing mostly for comfort. And yet, even then, I was already shaping my style around an image—in this era, a sporty one.

Nearly a decade later, my sister and I went back to that exact spot. I started scrolling through my online albums, trying to find that photo so we could recreate it. I struck the same pose, but my hair was down this time, and I was wearing a cotton striped maxi dress, wondering if the stripes made me look too big. What had happened to the girl I'd been with Mamaw, sitting next to Lucille Ball's statue in Palm Springs? The one who boarded the plane caring what other people thought, but not letting it change her? The one I'd captured on film without even realizing it?

Like all the girls around me, I suppose, I started off seeing myself as the main character of my life story, but phrases like "girls are catty" or "boys are better at sports" planted seeds of doubt. Little by little, I stopped seeing the world through my own eyes and started seeing myself through the eyes of others, shaping who I was to match what I thought they wanted.

By eleven, that world had already begun to mold me. But I wasn't shrinking yet—I hadn't learned to make myself smaller. Back then, I was an athlete, a tomboy in my purest form, wearing my reputation like a badge of honor, as certain of myself as the stars scattered across the hills behind us.

Unwritten Rules

O ver the years, I became enamored by a culture that somehow convinced me that I needed more than sports shorts and sneakers to make me whole. That having 450 items in my closet still wasn't enough. I wasn't the only one; many of us came to believe the message we got from influencers on social media, who showed us a highly curated part of their lives and capitalized on that—more definitely is more.

However, this wasn't always the norm. Juliet Schor, a sociology professor at Boston College, talks about this shift, saying:

The new consumerism is characterized by the fact that people are buying more things, and more expensive things, not because they need them or even because they particularly want them, but because they are continually upping the ante on what they consider an acceptable standard of living.

I was living this shift—my twenties were a blur of fast-fashion purchases from places like H&M. Despite the overflowing closet, I often felt like I had nothing to wear. My personal style was buried under a mountain of "shoulds" and rigid rules that I had carried since childhood. Shopping was my attempt at rediscovering it, or at the very least, a fun distraction.

After joining a startup that embraced the capsule wardrobe philosophy, I began to experience a different perspective. My colleagues had limited wardrobes, and each showcased a unique style that felt authentic and personal, like their own mini brand. A well-worn denim jacket became more than an item of clothing. They wore it time and again, telling a story of love for well-weathered classics.

The concept wasn't exactly new. In the 1970s, Susie Faux created a way of building a smaller wardrobe with only your favorite items, calling it a "capsule." But today, it pushes against everything we've been sold about what it means to live a good life or to have any semblance of style.

Yet, I watched Chris, a colleague, turn his morning coffee ritual into an art form, and I began to see new possibilities. He was meticulous and unhurried as he measured and monitored the water temperature, pouring it steadily over the coffee grounds. He was deliberate and calm—a stark contrast to my fast-paced, drip-machine, more-is-better approach to life.

And I started listening to others like me, who were overwhelmed by their wardrobes, never feeling "put together," constantly trying to shop their way out of a problem that seemed to only get worse. Instead of feeling freedom, they felt weighed down by the sheer number of choices. I saw that I wasn't the only one trapped in an endless cycle, searching for a way out.

Our overstuffed closets were clearly more than spaces to store our clothes. They were like mirrors that showed how culture sneaks in, getting us to buy into the stories of who we ought to be without us realizing these aren't the clothes (or careers or lives) we actually want.

We often let culture dictate what we should love. But if we're not careful, we may find ourselves living lives designed by others rather than crafting our own.

Building a capsule wardrobe taught me to pause and consider what I liked, apart from what's popular. It reminded me of what it is I love—something I had forgotten to do as I became an adult. Editing my closet wasn't merely about making space; it reawakened parts of myself that had been asleep. The parts that no longer needed to fit in or be someone I wasn't.

I realized that much of what I'd gathered wasn't for me. Otherwise, why did the fitted maxi dress still have a tag on it? Why did anything in a pastel go unworn season after season? No matter how much I wanted to be that girl, I wasn't. I dreamed of wearing the preppy polo shirts from the J.Crew catalog, but that wasn't me—and it never would be. Just like I'd never be the girl who effortlessly pulled off flowy floral dresses the way my free-spirited friends did.

I needed to stop chasing who I thought I should be and start embracing who I was. That meant clearing away the clutter—the expectations, the opinions, the endless lists of "shoulds" so I could finally see what was left. The real me, underneath it all.

As I applied these principles to my wardrobe, I couldn't help but wonder—what if I approached my life the same way? What if I learned to let go before reaching for more? To choose intention over impulse, quality over quantity? To focus on creating instead of constantly consuming? That last one—that's the hardest.

Figuring out what I loved was always at the core. It changed the way I saw everything—what I owned, what I valued, and how I made decisions. More than just a way to simplify my closet, it became a clear and reliable guide for reshaping how I lived. And it all started with recognizing the clutter I was still holding on to—and learning to finally let it go.

PART TWO

Clutter

Letting Go of What Doesn't Fit

> Can you remember
> who you were before
> the world told you
> who you should be?

— CHARLES BUKOWSKI

Need *for* Control

WHEN I THOUGHT ABOUT MY BODY GROWING up, it was all about height, speed, and agility. The measurements that used to be a sign of my athleticism morphed into numbers on a scale in college. The story ran deep. I didn't want to be the woman who "let herself go." And the stats on eating disorders among female athletes would indicate that I wasn't the only one who struggled with this story.

Running a tight ship became my go-to solution. The control it took to eat this, not that. No bread or dairy. All bread. All dairy. Plants only. Meat this week. All of which left me weary.

The cultural conversation has since moved toward body positivity, introducing another story about "loving your body" to our collection. But I can't love my body any more than I love my mind. It's as much a part of me as my right eye or left toe—each a piece of the whole.

Adding more stories didn't help, but removing the unnecessary ones did. I am learning to listen to what my body needs instead of training myself to ignore it at every turn. I am no longer blindly replacing my thoughts with the next trendy diet someone on the internet offers up.

Have you ever noticed the voice that shames you for eating chocolate ice cream in a waffle cone or the one that criticizes you for enjoying a small bag of Doritos? I've let the voice that shames, rushes, or berates me guide my decision-making while second-guessing the other, more loving voice most of my life.

Of course, changing this way of living has kept me from starting my diet on Monday or losing the extra ten pounds I'd been saying I would lose for a decade. I had to let go of the idea that no future version of me looked any different from how I looked right now, and I was okay with that.

Turning down the world's noise when it gets loud has taken time. Regardless of my new perspective, Pinterest keeps flaunting those "10-day abs" pins, jeans keep changing sizes, and influencers...be influencing. I'd like to say this has been an easy transition, but the more accurate word that describes the journey is that it's taken practice.

I never really enjoyed practicing back when I played basketball, but I understood it was necessary to reach a point where shooting three-pointers felt effortless. It's been fifteen years since I played competitively, yet I can still pick up a ball and shoot with the same form I had, as if I'd never stopped. I aspire for that kind of mastery, where the skill of figuring out how to eat is so ingrained it becomes a part of who I am.

Today, when negative thoughts enter, I treat them more like old friends who popped in for a visit. I see them, say hi, and let them go their merry way rather than handing over the steering wheel so they can drive my life. This path hasn't been without a few detours. I can't say I'll ever have this one fully figured out. The current is so wide and strong, omnipresent.

But I am in a much better place. The girl who once found reassurance in daily weigh-ins hasn't stepped on a scale in over seven years. I can write this paragraph without guilt, savoring every flaky, sweet bite of an almond croissant.

The same way I clung to clothes I no longer wore, I held on to beliefs, habits, and expectations that no longer fit me.

The pressure to find something to wear mirrored the pressure to maintain the perfect weight. My closet was just the most visible example of a much bigger problem: I had filled my life with things I thought I needed, yet none of them gave me the calm I was searching for.

What the world won't tell you is that when we finally let go, we begin to find who we really are.

The Inner Critic

GRADUATING IN 2009, I STEPPED INTO A WORLD that bore little resemblance to the one I had prepared for. The nation was grappling with a full-on financial crisis, the media labeling it the largest economic crash since the Great Depression. Not only were managers not hiring for entry-level marketing positions, entire marketing departments were being dismantled overnight.

I sent out résumé after résumé, each one disappearing into what felt like an endless void. With every unanswered application, a little piece of my identity seemed to unravel. The security that being an athlete had provided—a familiar safety net—was gone. The script I had followed my entire life—work hard, earn good grades, stack up achievements—had always led to the next milestone. Now, I had followed it to the end, only to find nothing waiting for me. I was no longer *the athlete*, but I wasn't yet *a young professional*. I was lost in the crowd, searching for a new role to play.

Without any playbook to guide me, I clung to what I knew—hard work, grit, and the belief that if I could push through, things would eventually fall into place. Still, what was I pushing toward? Since I didn't know which direction to go in, I did what I had always done: I went "shopping" for a new path, collecting roles, taking advice from those more qualified, and gathering expectations. Not realizing that later they'd pile up, so much clutter, I filled my life with the things I thought I *should* be doing—things that looked like success on paper. Even though the hustle mentality had already run me into the ground once before, I still believed it was the key. It had worked in sports. It had worked in the classroom. So why wouldn't it work now?

One evening, I sat on the couch, a mess of tears, utterly defeated after yet another job rejection. I was supposed to be kicking off the best years of my life—settling into a new city, starting a marriage, using my degree. Instead, I found myself at what felt like rock bottom, smack in the middle of a quarter-life crisis. My husband, Colin, who had a knack for solving problems when I was stuck, stepped in with a challenge. He introduced me to this thing called a blog (yes, in 2009, blogs were still "a thing") and challenged me to write for ninety days straight. I wasn't one to back down from a challenge. To give you an idea, I decided to quit drinking pop (soda, for you non-Midwesterners) on the heels of a thirty-day New Year's resolution in 1999. I haven't had a sip since. I leaned into work again—but this time, it was different. I wasn't an athlete anymore, but I was starting to see myself as something else: an entrepreneur.

One day, after scrolling through a magazine online, I ran across Ralph Lauren's 2009 Spring "Ready to Wear" Collection. There was a beautiful model, blond hair flowing, a wide-brimmed hat tilted off to the side. She walked confidently in sparkle harem pants that resembled the huge drop-crotch ones that MC Hammer wore back in the day. Underneath the photo, the caption hailed them as the year's newest trend. I thought otherwise. In fact, I thought this was a flashing sign showing just how out of touch the fashion industry was. Which gave me everything I needed to begin writing. The blog was called *Reality Chic*. Its manifesto? "Because real people don't wear sparkle pants to Olive Garden." It was a telling sign in itself, revealing just how "middle-class fancy" I was.

My blog had been live for only a few weeks when I received my first internet critique. I couldn't imagine who was reading it, let alone commenting. When I was notified that "1 comment has been made," I hurried to my blog.

Nervous energy filled my entire body. My fingers were damp with the kind of icy sweat that comes with uncertainty. I opened the comment, and it read...

"You have a dog face."

Yep, you read that right. The first comment I ever received online told me I had a dog face. An actual human being took time out of their day to tell me that.

I would like to say I was prepared for the criticism, though is one ever really prepared? I was mortified, embarrassed, and in tears. Not only was it my first comment, it was sitting at the bottom of the article for all of my friends and family to see.

I slammed my computer shut. Far more than I feared having a dog face (dogs are super cute), I was terrified that the voice of my inner critic wasn't just in my head anymore. Now, it was out in the open, coming at me from a stranger on the internet. And as much as I wanted to brush it off, I couldn't. Because it echoed voices I already knew too well—the teacher who laughed, Allie's mom who accused, my coach who scolded. It seemed safer to stay quiet than to risk confusion or upsetting someone else.

I had done what everyone says you're supposed to do: put yourself out there, take a risk, go after something bigger. The truth was, I didn't even know why I was doing it. I wanted success, sure, but I couldn't have told you what that actually meant for me. I was going faster and further without a clear direction, and that uncertainty made every hit feel heavier.

I've never quite gotten used to how often women's looks are used to dismiss what they have to say. If I'm being honest, it wasn't the insult itself that stung the most. It was the feeling that they were trying to put me in my place.

And the hardest part? I wasn't even sure where my place was.

Playing *the* Part

ONE PATH FORWARD WAS BECOMING PART OF THE unfolding of influencer culture in the new digital era. There had always been storytelling. Traditional gatekeepers held it. Publishers for books. Journalists for media. But blogging was a new foray, and the internet served as a platform allowing "real" people to share "real" experiences. After hitting publish, anyone from anywhere could unleash their opinion for the rest of the internet to find.

I watched the power, once hoarded by a few, transition into the hands of the many, sparking a mini revolution.

Fashion was being flipped on its head by people who were once mere spectators, but who were now being photographed on their walk to the iconic Lincoln Center for Mercedes-Benz Fashion Week, because the clothes they were wearing influenced what retailers were producing for the racks.

Prominent figures we know today, like Glennon Doyle, Tim Ferriss, Gary Vaynerchuk, Joanna Gaines, and Ayesha Curry, started humbly by blogging on their computer screens. Platforms such as *Refinery29* and *The Huffington Post* gained recognition as legitimate sources. Whether equipped with traditional credentials or not, their influence on politics and women's issues was irrefutable. The floodgates were flung wide open, and the current was irreversible. Women were now telling their stories and growing audiences, prompting brands to take notice. These were the days when Blogger, Tumblr, and WordPress ruled the internet, and I, a girl from rural Indiana, could get credentials to attend New York Fashion Week.

I partnered with various brands to explore what collaboration between bloggers and companies could look like in this new world. In exchange, I received free clothing, gift cards, a smartphone, and occasional payments. I was staring at the forefront of Web 2.0, and I saw the beauty of it all. How I could be part of righting an industry once fraught with unattainable beauty standards. The days when the only images we saw were of poreless, photoshopped models were over. Influencers gave a fresh perspective.

I'd been blogging for over a year when I got an email inviting me to come to New York City for a guest appearance on a reality TV show called *All on the Line* with Joe Zee (formerly the creative director of *Elle* magazine). After the initial shock and a quick Google search to check if I was being scammed, I immediately started thinking about what I should wear. Who goes on TV without agonizing about the "right" outfit when your face and body will be magnified on a big screen? Not me, I can tell you that.

I began typing, "What do you wear on TV?" And, voilà, the wisdom of the internet delivered, pointing me to blue as the most TV-friendly color. I chose a solid, unpatterned blue shirt and my trusty black skinny jeans. Classic and safe, this is a no-fail outfit. Why? Because the internet said so. That's why.

On the big day, I woke up at 5:00 a.m. to make sure I'd catch the bus on time, like I always did before heading into New York. I flipped the TV onto The Weather Channel, finding comfort in the meteorologists who were already awake and told me it would be a hot one. I got in the car and drove off to the Scranton Greyhound Station with my messenger bag and my neck pillow. It was the same bus route I had taken to New York City months before when I took an unpaid internship at WeightWatchers to gain some experience while I couldn't find a job. This time, I was tracking the amount of hours it took. Three hours there. Three hours back.

Arriving in New York City always felt like stepping onto the set of a movie. The journey through the darkness of the Lincoln Tunnel, suddenly bursting into the bright lights and bustling activity of the city—it was exhilarating. I remember stepping out of Port Authority, gazing up at the New York Times Building, and feeling like I had finally made it. Being in New York was once a distant dream for a girl from Indiana. The city's energy hit me first, followed by a wave of scorching ninety-five-degree heat, thanks to all the concrete and asphalt. With no driver waiting to whisk me away, I was quickly reminded that I hadn't quite "made it, made it" yet.

I started walking toward 1271 Avenue of the Americas, that iconic forty-eight-story skyscraper where Time Inc. once was located, which happened to be where we were filming. I don't know if it was the temperature or the fact I had little experience hailing a cab, but I could not summon one if my life depended on it. After a sweaty thirteen-and-a-half-block trek, I ducked into a café near the building only to look down and see that I had sweated through my entire shirt. And not just a little. I'm talking about pit stains rivaling the size of Montana. Blue was not forgiving. Cue inner panic.

I couldn't show up for my TV debut with my arms glued to my sides in a sweat-soaked terror. I envisioned watching myself with friends and family, stuttering over my words while focused on nothing but hiding sweat under my armpits. So I decided to improvise. After weeks of preparing what I would wear, I threw it out the window in a hot minute—looking for the closest retailer, I spotted an Anthropologie across from Rockefeller Center.

I've never walked so fast, looked so conspicuous, and been so willing to drop a cool one hundred dollars while shopping. I desperately searched for a shirt that screamed TV-ready. Fifteen minutes later, I emerged victorious with an ivory top, not blue but stain-free. I walked back to 1271 Avenue of the Americas just in time to hear Joe Zee tell me that I looked fabulous. I wished we were close enough so I could give him the backstory. Rest assured, we were not.

I found myself in an extra conference room, surrounded by a few fellow bloggers, eagerly awaiting the producer's signal. The room was filled with anticipation and last-minute mirror checks. The producer came in one last time, giving us a clear directive: We must love the designer's looks or hate them—no in-between. According to her, deliberation didn't make for good TV. Right then I took in the sheer spectacle of it all.

Reality versus Reality TV.

It was almost comical, knowing that hours earlier, I was a hot, sweaty mess, panicking in an Anthropologie dressing room. Now, I was playing a cool, calm, collected, know-it-all judge on a TV show.

I did not become a reality TV star. Nor did Joe Zee and I become best friends. But that day will always stay with me. Because if I learned anything, it's this: What you see isn't always what you get. Perception can be convincing—it can look and feel like the truth—but that doesn't mean it is. And if you spend too much time trying to fit into a version of reality that was never yours to begin with, you just might miss out on the life that actually is.

Waiting *for* Approval

O NE EVENING, AFTER AN UNUSUAL NUMBER OF pitches landed in my inbox offering only free clothes, I began exploring what bridging the gap between brands and bloggers could look like.

Before I knew it, I was a first-time founder attempting to raise money for my newly formed startup, an influencer network designed before influencers were making a living through marketing. It wasn't long before I found myself vying for the attention of investors, attempting to impress them with my latest elevator pitch and finding creative ways to get in front of them.

This was pre-*Lean In*. There was no #GirlBoss or #WomenInTech movement. It was a time when a comment like "the market you're going after isn't big enough" was still code for "you're targeting women." I wasn't yet privy to the challenges of being a female founder. I still maintained a level of naive confidence that the world offered me every bit of what it offered my male counterparts. I started to see that I was not just one of the guys. My gender was a factor I had rarely considered.

After college, I started following Gary Vee on social media. He was one of the few people who understood the reality of young people struggling to find a job after the economic crash of 2008. He preached about not following the crowd and putting in the work. Investors didn't network or respond to emails. From what I could tell, the only way to get in was if you had connections or an Ivy League background—neither of which I did. When I learned that he was a successful investor in his own right, I did what any follower of Gary Vee would do: I took his advice.

Gary's birthday was coming up, and he had welcomed a new baby. He made his passion for the New York Jets well-known on social media. After a little digging for his address (not advised), I got on Etsy and ordered a New York Jets-themed diaper cake with our startup's Executive Summary attached to it. It was scheduled to be delivered to his doorstep...so I thought.

Hearing crickets, I sent a follow-up email.

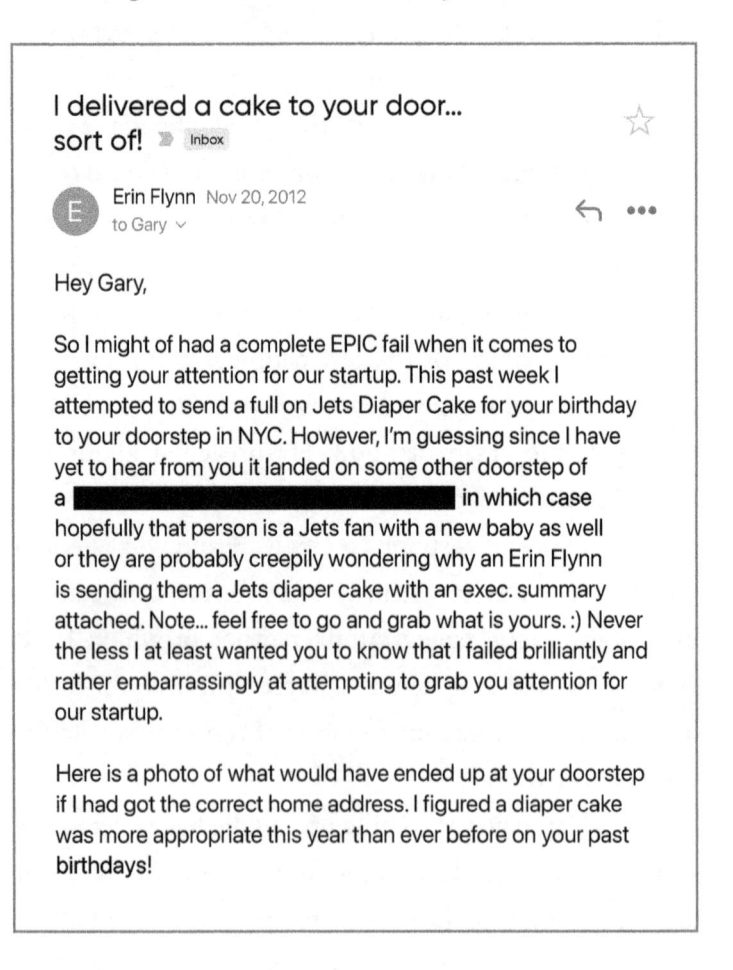

> **I delivered a cake to your door... sort of!** Inbox
>
> **Erin Flynn** Nov 20, 2012
> to Gary
>
> Hey Gary,
>
> So I might of had a complete EPIC fail when it comes to getting your attention for our startup. This past week I attempted to send a full on Jets Diaper Cake for your birthday to your doorstep in NYC. However, I'm guessing since I have yet to hear from you it landed on some other doorstep of a ▇▇▇▇▇▇▇▇▇▇▇▇▇▇▇▇▇▇▇▇▇▇ in which case hopefully that person is a Jets fan with a new baby as well or they are probably creepily wondering why an Erin Flynn is sending them a Jets diaper cake with an exec. summary attached. Note... feel free to go and grab what is yours. :) Never the less I at least wanted you to know that I failed brilliantly and rather embarrassingly at attempting to grab you attention for our startup.
>
> Here is a photo of what would have ended up at your doorstep if I had got the correct home address. I figured a diaper cake was more appropriate this year than ever before on your past birthdays!

Within days, I received this...

> **Re: I delivered a cake to your door... sort of!** Inbox
>
> **gary vaynerchuk** Nov 28, 2012
> to Erin, Nathan
>
> OH man I dont live there :(Erin lets talk in jan come see me for 15 minutes based on your efforts!

Great! But there was one problem—I didn't live in New York. By then, we had returned to Cincinnati for my husband's job. But after receiving this email, I packed my bags and made an impromptu visit to meet Gary Vee at Vaynerchuk Media's offices in New York City.

When I arrived at his company's offices, I was surprised to meet a soft-spoken Gary, different from the feisty alter ego I'd seen on Facebook. He was considerate, taking far more than fifteen minutes to listen to my pitch and answer any questions. Gary didn't invest that day, and to be honest, I'm not even sure I asked. I wanted to get his approval, hoping his level of status would rub off on us, calming any fears I had about whether or not our startup would succeed.

Pitching to investors often felt like navigating a delicate dance—one I could never quite master. I craved their approval, their reassurance. They wanted a return. They fired off questions, and I scrambled to anticipate the answers they wanted to hear. The truth was, neither of us was completely honest about why we were really there.

Because they weren't looking for the whole truth. They were looking for a story they could believe in—one that made their decision feel safe, predictable, worth the risk. And for too long, I had done the same in my own life. I'd packaged my story, polished the edges, made it more palatable. But the real value—the real return—was never in the version that sounded best. It was in the one that was real.

Navigating *the* "-Isms"

EVERY YEAR, I TAKE A TRIP TO FLORIDA WITH MY family. It's a ten-hour drive, typically filled with unpredictable traffic. However, we've learned over the years to keep Google Maps open, not because we don't know the way but to help us find alternate routes when the traffic gets too heavy. It's fascinating to observe how many drivers remain gridlocked, oblivious to the same tool they carry in their pockets that could provide them with a more stress-free journey.

It's a striking metaphor for life. We're all aiming for a similar destination, trying to live our best life, but life will throw up roadblocks, many in the form of one "-ism" or another—racism, sexism, elitism, for example. Some people find a way to stay open even so, savoring the journey and finding such deep satisfaction in the scenic route that they inspire others to join in. Others remain closed off, believing that travel is destined to be a grueling slog, which only leaves them drained and irritable, empty when they finally arrive at their destination.

My papaw always had this saying: "Life isn't fair." He'd bring this gem out whenever the grandkids complained about what went wrong at practice or school. I was never a huge fan of the phrase as a little kid. I wanted to believe in a world where the good guys always won and everything eventually balanced. Now that I'm older, I see the wisdom in his words. Life is rarely about fairness. Racism, sexism, and the hoarding of wealth and power make that clear. And yet, the story of the American Dream still resonates—the belief that we can change our circumstances if we work hard enough.

For me, building a startup was my way of testing that idea. It was my escape from the traditional nine-to-five. And if there was any industry where success had a clear scorecard, it was the startup world. In the Midwest, entrepreneurs were gathering, driven by a pioneer spirit I could feel. For the first time in my career, I felt like I belonged.

NAVIGATING THE "-ISMS"

My husband grew up in Cincinnati. For me, everything was brand-new—I had never lived in the city before. We had moved there after a short stint out East, and I was taking it all in—the neighborhoods, the food, and the way people talked about their high schools as if they were colleges. I was excited to befriend a fellow founder whose startup was a few steps ahead of mine. While brutal in his delivery, I appreciated his honesty and wanted nothing more than someone to show me the ropes and illuminate the road ahead.

With the scent of chicken in the air and games blasting in the background, I joined him for dinner at Buffalo Wild Wings. When the waiter brought the first round of drinks, we shared the pains of running our businesses. Then, as smoothly as he downed his beer, his words poured out.

"I would never invest in a woman. They're too emotional."

Gulp.

I wasn't asking for money. He didn't have any. And that's not what this dinner was about. I leaned in for clarification: "So, you wouldn't invest in me even though we're friends?"

"No," he casually repeated, "women are too emotional to run a company." (Punching him in the face was one of the nicer thoughts that ran through my mind at the time.)

Unfortunately, his brutal words did, in fact, illuminate the path ahead. Different voices, same shade. Like when I was told, "I'm glad you don't have kids. When women have kids, their priorities shift, and they're not as focused on work." Or, "Once you have a boyfriend it will be a distraction to playing basketball." As though to say being a whole person isn't an option for you, though men have been doing it for centuries.

Comments like these piled up over the years, slowly creeping into my thoughts and quietly putting up roadblocks. I started to believe that feelings were bad things. That showing vulnerability somehow equated to weakness.

But what I was really learning was that life wasn't fair. It just wasn't. And no matter how much I wished it were different, the truth remained—sexism wasn't fair, but it existed. The question was, could I acknowledge it without letting it have the final say? Better yet, could I hold that truth while still carving my own path forward?

Fighting Sexism

A FEW MONTHS EARLIER, I HAD TRIED TO RAISE A seed round of financing to kick-start our new company. I applied to a few accelerators to secure capital to launch our startup. Accelerators were new mentor-based programs intended to give startups both support and money. There was a catch—if we got in, we'd have to move to where the program was located for three months—but it felt like a small price to pay for the financial security.

I had my eyes on one accelerator near where we were living. I stood outside looking at a newly renovated urban building with Italianate architecture in downtown

Cincinnati. Months earlier, after befriending a few entrepreneurs, I was invited to work out of the building before the next class of founders was selected. My desk was in a tiny corner facing the wall on the second floor, but it beat working from home by myself. Until we officially secured funding, my other cofounders needed to work their day jobs before joining full-time.

I took a long breath before I entered, trying to release the nerves bubbling inside me. I hated the stress of presenting. It always felt as if I were putting on a performance, but we had made it to the final interview for this year's class. It was our best shot at getting an initial investment for a new company.

We walked up the winding wooden staircase to the second floor, past my desk, where we sat side by side at a long conference table. Three guys were firing off question after question. We took turns answering, demonstrating that we were both capable. Then came the curveball we hadn't prepared for: "Why isn't he the CEO?"

My male cofounder and I locked eyes. A long pause passed between us as we looked for the right words. I launched into an explanation, avoiding the heart of the question. I spoke about our target demographic and how we were attracting women bloggers writing about beauty and fashion—something I had direct experience in. I was

FIGHTING SEXISM

trying hard, channeling every ounce of effort to impress them with my qualifications.

I left that interview not understanding what had happened. I walked confidently through the entrance but left doubting far more than our acceptance. Up until this point, I had been the one doing most of the pitching and most of the speaking since I was living proof of the market we were entering. I started to get the sense that it wasn't me investors wanted to hear from. I had always believed that hard work guaranteed success. That story was starting to crumble. Securing funding wasn't up to me anymore. It was in the hands of three older white men.

It felt like being back out on the playground; I had to prove, once again, that a girl could hang in a "guy's sport." Only now there was no hoop shoot contest or Title IX to level the playing field. Just an industry that entrusted men to create the same opportunities for people who didn't look like them or come from similar backgrounds, hoping they would be kind enough to open doors.

My "friend's" comment had come to life in a way I least expected. That year, we were not accepted. Noticeably, neither were any other female CEOs. Later that winter we joined an accelerator in Detroit, receiving our first round of funding. The irony couldn't have been more stark.

It was run by a female.

83

Playing Girls *vs.* Boys

GROWING UP, 1 WAS CONDITIONED NOT AS female or male but as an athlete. Receiving typical masculine messaging, coaches encouraged me to be "bigger in the post," "stronger by lifting weights," and "more aggressive on defense." Quaint, quiet, or passive never crossed my mind. Small had no place on the court.

Of course, sexist undertones were present: snide remarks about the girls' team versus the boys' team pulling more of a crowd to watch. Or the lengths we'd go to appear feminine while playing so as not to be perceived as "butch." Still, my talent and skills took precedence, even with a French braid. All the years I spent being coached by men and playing against boys gave me no qualms about entering into the male-dominated tech industry. Naively, I thought the startup ecosystem would be like sports.

I was aware that sexism existed, but if I'm being honest, I assumed it was something that "other women" had to deal with. It's mortifying to admit that deep down, I thought they must have done something to contribute to it. It wasn't until I found myself in a meeting with an investor who would address only my husband, refusing to acknowledge I was the one pitching, that I recognized I had it all wrong.

"Athlete" was a shield that had protected me for more than a quarter of my life. Without my jersey, that aspect of my identity now receded into the shadows. Investors saw me for who I appeared to be on the surface—a twenty-five-year-old white woman. I was no longer an equal.

Being an athlete gave me an edge that I couldn't ever put my finger on. Without really thinking about it, I had figured out how to play the game. Dropping mentions of sports or my athletic past early in conversations turned out to be a tool I learned to leverage. Instantly I'd earn more respect than I could otherwise. Like I wasn't one of the girls if they could see me as one of the guys.

Gender exacerbated the already-complicated power dynamics between young founders like me and older investors who held the power, though no one was talking about it yet. We weren't silent by choice, but there was no HR department in the startup world, and the wave of the Me Too movement in Silicon Valley wouldn't make the issue obvious until years later. I was on my own, trying to navigate how gender played a factor in reaching my goals.

There's so much I would do differently today, including walking out of that meeting. But that's the thing about being caught off guard—you never see it coming. At first, I wanted to blame everyone—the guys, the sports industry, the startup scene. And for a while, I did. But sitting in that frustration only kept me stuck.

I kept trying to push my way down a road that was never built for me, convinced that if I just tried harder, I could make it work. But some paths aren't meant to be forced. Instead of exhausting myself trying to prove I belonged, I started looking for another way—one where hard work felt life-giving, not depleting. One where I wasn't striving to prove my worth but living from it. A path that wasn't handed to me, but one I had the freedom to create.

Working *Harder*

REMEMBER IT LIKE IT WAS YESTERDAY. THE MOMENT I realized the company I loved was dead. By then, Cladwell had been through several changes including launching a new app in the app store, and I'd stepped up as cofounder and CMO.

I had spent time, money, and energy intertwining who I was with the company. I had fought for it and convinced myself that if I just worked harder, if I just pushed through one more stress-filled moment, I could keep it from becoming the cautionary tale of my first startup.

But the truth was, I already knew it was slipping away.

We had taken on an investor out of sheer desperation—bad money, but necessary to survive. I knew at the time that it came with consequences, that we were giving away more than equity. But I still believed we could make it work.

Then came the meeting. The same old debate, the same old tension—this time for three days and with more stakes. My cofounder, who at the time was the CEO, sat across from me. We were locked in another tug-of-war, but instead of arguing further, something inside me shifted. I could feel it: The company I loved was gone. Not officially, not publicly, but I wasn't holding the reins anymore. And maybe I never really had been.

I leaned back in my chair, staring at the dull gray storage cabinets. For months, I had been grasping, strategizing, hoping. But this was the moment I saw it for what it was. The pressure of trying to be a billion-dollar unicorn was crushing our mission, sending us spiraling.

The grief hit me before the reality did. Not just for the business, but for the version of myself who believed this ride could last forever. Who thought that with enough effort and belief I could change the trajectory of something that no longer belonged to her. Founder versus founder, we argued about what to do next. It was me against him. My hands were clammy, adrenaline coursing through my veins. I was outmanned, literally. The pull to be and grow like other tech giants was drowning our business. Sure, the business could have been worth billions.

But eventually, we went bust.

For months, I had feared losing the work I had tied my identity to. But now, I could see—I had already lost it.

Working *More*

BACK IN 1972, TITLE IX KICKED OPEN THE DOOR for girls in sports. By the early 2000s, I was growing up thinking that any opportunity available to boys was as much mine, including future career opportunities.

According to Pew Research, work has almost become a new kind of religion, promising a purpose-driven identity and a sense of belonging. Some have dubbed it "workism." An article in *The Atlantic* describes it as the gospel of work: "The decline of traditional faith in America has coincided with an explosion of new atheisms. Some worship beauty, others political identities, and others their children. Everyone worships something, and workism is one of the most potent new religions vying for followers."

The belief in workism is that work isn't only necessary for economic reasons—it's central to one's identity and life's purpose. This aligns with the old American Dream narrative that hard work guarantees upward mobility, a notion that's obsessed America with material success for over a century.

Back in the mid-1100s, French Abbot Bernard of Clairvaux first said, "The road to hell is paved with good intentions." Today, women of my generation have grown up with work woven tightly into our identities, much like it was for men in previous generations. We were sold on the idea that career success was key to happiness and financial success. But the reality that "equal opportunity" didn't mean "equal outcome" hit hard as I faced the facts. Female founders like myself receive only 2 percent of startup funding, and women hold just 25 percent of C-level positions in corporations, earning roughly eighty-two cents for every dollar earned by men. The higher I climbed, the more I realized the prize was flawed from the start.

Henry David Thoreau once warned, "The mass of men lead lives of quiet desperation." I feared that many women, including myself, were now treading the same path. The misleading narrative was too ingrained to easily identify any single liar or source of misinformation. No one explicitly told me to value work above all else—it was the air I breathed.

Much like how I once thought a bigger closet meant better style, I believed more money and success would lead to a better life.

And as the digital era birthed what's known as the creator economy, I thought I'd find both there. It's promise—empowering not only millennials but also Gen Z, turning passions into viable income streams through scalable technology and offering opportunities for passive income like never before. The story? Work less and live more.

It sounded good to me. In 2019, I was one of many hurried, caffeinated, email-checking, notifications-always-on types of people. Life had been a blur after taking over the company, constantly on 2x speed.

I had been searching for a different way to run my company, one that didn't require the relentless hustle pushed by startup culture. The creator economy offered a trendy story that promised more freedom and flexibility. I jumped on board, trying this new approach like trying on a new outfit. I set up systems, hired a team, and even brought on a business coach to make sure I could step back from the day-to-day. Finally, I thought I'd found relief.

"Get passive income," they said. "It'll be fun," they said.

Chasing *the* American Dream

WHEN THE PANDEMIC HIT, MY MANTRA—LIKE everyone else's—became: slow down.

I went from having a filled calendar to no plans at all. I'd be remiss to tell you that, sickness aside, I secretly thought the change in speed was the very reckoning many of us, myself included, needed. It was as if the universe had conspired to enforce the slowdown I had long advocated for in fashion.

As days became weeks and weeks stretched into months, the pandemic stripped away layers of my life, routines, and activities. Like clutter in my closet, it revealed another uncomfortable truth: If doing more wasn't the answer, doing less wasn't, either.

During this period, my company turned a corner from being cash-strapped to steady and profitable. I started drawing a salary and even hired people I was thrilled to work with. You could say I was living the new American Dream: financially free in a company I loved without being tethered to "the man." But, to be honest, something about that dream felt off.

One day, tears streamed down my face during a call with one of the few investors I'd brought on board since becoming CEO. There was no acting cool. Any coolness I had flew out the window when he leaned in and simply asked, "How are you doing?" I was on the verge of shouting, "Not good!"

On paper, I had reached the mountain top, turning the business around. I could grab coffee with friends midday, vacation in Florida, and play pickleball with my husband in the afternoons. It was like a scene from *The 4-Hour Workweek*. And yet I was miserable, questioning why this tale of financial freedom didn't feel like the fairytale I'd been promised.

Desperate for relief, I called my business coach, begging her to tell me exactly what to do with my newfound free time: "Spend more time with the people that matter most to you."

I let out a heavy sigh.

When she said those words, I felt an immense weight on my shoulders. I knew what I was supposed to say back: "Great, I'd love to spend more time with my husband and son." Truthfully, it was a lie. Don't get me wrong. I love my husband and son more than anything in this world. However, I feel like I already spend ample time with my family; plus they, too, have lives of their own. Ones that don't require me to sit next to them at all hours of the day. Her guidance followed a familiar theme that resonates with a lesson the pandemic underscored for all of us: Having an abundance of time isn't the silver bullet we thought it once was.

I've seen my parents' generation realize that happiness doesn't come from more stuff. And I've wrestled with my own generation's belief that more free time is the key. If working more isn't the answer, working less isn't, either. In my relentless pursuit of the new American Dream, which promised more time, I overlooked a crucial question: How would I use it?

If success wasn't measured by accumulating more things or having plenty of time, then what was it really about?

Despite my allergy to the relentless pace of startup culture, I was equally annoyed by the emptiness of having nothing to look forward to. Content yet devoid of creativity. Was this the kind of desperation Thoreau had so eloquently articulated?

Betty Friedan hit the nail on the head back in the '60s when she said, "The only way for a woman, as for a man, to find herself, to know herself as a person, is by creative work of her own. There is no other way."

It seemed like modern women had two options: dive headfirst into the relentless hustle of startup culture or settle into the often soul-sucking routines of corporate America. The problem wasn't just the work itself—it was the stories absorbed about what work *should* look like. I had simply traded one form of discontent for another, exhaustion for disengagement, mistaking it for a solution. Too hurried to stop to ask myself what *I* actually wanted and too quick to take another person's advice for what worked for them.

By all accounts, I had it all—time, money, freedom. Yet, I felt empty. Work matters. It's an outlet for creativity, a way to use our skills to serve others. But it should serve *us*—not consume us.

Without meaningful work, I wasn't struggling, but I was drifting—floating without direction or purpose. In my work, as in my closet, it was easy enough to identify *what* I loved. After all, that's how I ended up in fashion. But figuring out *why*? That was harder.

Burning *Out*

One afternoon, while hanging out with my sister-in-law, I made a joke about my dog-paddling skills. I was never taught to swim formally, which made it entertaining for everyone else watching me at a pool party. She launched into a story about her old lifeguarding days, and I couldn't help but hear the striking resemblance to my life as an entrepreneur.

She described how the kids often struggled to float in the water, counterproductively trying to work really hard to do it. The harder they fought, the worse it got. She would tell them a short story or make up a silly song to get them to relax. Keeping steady and calm was the key to unlocking the ability to float.

It hit me: The fundamentals of swimming sounded all too similar to running the company. I'd lost count of the number of times I had tried harder—an anxious effort to find the right marketing channel to attract new users, make viral content, send mass emails, or attempt to force more growth with paid ads. I was drowning in sweat equity and pulling under any poor soul brave enough to come save me from myself.

One of the earliest stories I told myself was about the value of hard work. When it comes to fight, flight, or freeze, fighting has always been my default. The constant, strenuous movement of fighting always makes me feel like I'm progressing. I was never shy about using phrases like, "I'm drowning," to describe the struggle.

Greg McKeown, author of *Effortless*, says, "Strangely, some of us respond to feeling exhausted and overwhelmed by vowing to work even harder and longer. It doesn't help that our culture glorifies burnout as a measure of success and self-worth. The implicit message is that if we aren't perpetually exhausted, we must not be doing enough. Those great things are reserved for those who bleed, for those who almost break. Crushing volume is somehow now the goal. Burnout is not a badge of honor."

This mindset followed me long after college. I believed that if the work didn't feel hard enough, it didn't count—that struggle was a necessary part of success. So I pushed myself, ignoring every warning sign, until my knees were so damaged that even the simplest movements brought pain. Eventually, the sport I once loved became something I could no longer bring myself to pick up.

Stepping in as CEO of Cladwell wasn't all that different. I continued to prove that I could keep the business alive, that I had what it took to turn things around. I did what I'd always done. I worked harder. I poured myself into it, convinced that effort alone could hold everything together. But just like before, I hit a wall.

The difference now? There was no final buzzer, no graduation day, no built-in finish line. Just the realization that if suffering was how I measured success, I'd inevitably run myself into the ground.

I didn't realize it was happening to me until I caught myself feeling nothing at all. The work I once loved felt like a weight, and yet, I kept pushing—because slowing down felt like failure. I was exhausted but had convinced myself this was what success looked like. Worried I'd fall behind. The thought of slowing down made me anxious, as if resting meant I was giving up.

But here's what no one tells you about burnout—it doesn't hit all at once. It creeps in quietly, disguised as ambition, as dedication. At first, it feels like pride, like you're proving yourself. Then, one day, you wake up and realize you don't recognize who you are anymore. The things that used to energize you now drain you. You stop feeling excited, and you start feeling numb. And the worst part? You don't know how to stop. My career wasn't a basketball season I had to push through. It was the rest of my life. It became clearer that the issue wasn't the work itself, just like the problem was never basketball.

It never is.

For so long, I thought success meant pushing harder, working longer, and proving I could handle whatever came my way. I believed struggle was just part of the deal—the price you paid to get where you wanted to go. But somewhere along the way, I found myself holding on to too many "shoulds," too many stories about what success *should* look like. And all that clutter was wearing me down.

That's where we get it wrong.

Moving forward isn't about just suffering our way through it—it's about recognizing the clutter we've been holding on to, the old narratives that no longer fit, so we can finally let them go. It's stepping into a rhythm that feels like home, where we learn to work *with* ourselves instead of against ourselves.

Because real success isn't about fighting the water. First, you have to learn to float.

Shrinking Yourself

THERE I WAS, CAUGHT MID-CONVERSATION, WHEN I ran into an old coach of mine. He asked me what I was up to these days, particularly curious about whether I worked from home. I began explaining how my entire team works remotely, but before I could go into detail, he interrupted me: "Oh... your team."

The unsaid words hung in the air. Had I said something wrong? Was I coming off as arrogant rather than descriptive? In a swift attempt to deflect any perceived overconfidence, I moved the conversation toward my husband's job—an area I could discuss openly and seemingly without judgment.

The exchange didn't really bother me until later that night. As I lay in bed, a familiar old phrase popped into my mind: "Too big for your britches." I hadn't thought about this old-timey saying in years, but it suddenly seemed relevant, though ridiculous—the idea of me, a fully grown woman, worrying about outgrowing my proverbial britches! It was so absurd.

While the terms "business owner" or "founder" accurately described my role, saying them out loud seemed to teeter on the brink of self-importance. I chose to distract and divert, a dance I realized I had done many times before over speaking the simple truth.

Talking about myself has never felt natural. It's like playing a game where I'm not quite sure of the rules. I've always wrestled with how to show up—confident and ambitious, yet still down-to-earth enough to connect with the people around me.

Recognizing how even the smallest interactions can make us feel small was the reminder I needed to see just how much I've grown. I'm not who I once was. Maybe it was never about being too big for my britches—but about realizing I'd outgrown them.

Seeking "*Success*"

THERE I WAS. CUDDLED UP ALONGSIDE MY KID, preparing to teach him a lesson, when a phrase spilled out of my mouth, "We can wait a little bit, or we can complain. I think waiting is the better choice."

I heard my voice repeating back to me as if from a slow-motion movie scene. Much of what I've explored in writing this book is how progress often provides only temporary relief. Like a dog chasing its tail, I believed that movement was the answer, but in reality, going the wrong direction was a matter of wearing myself down. As C.S. Lewis once said, " We all want progress. But progress means getting nearer to the place you want to be. And if you've taken a wrong turning, then to go forward does not get you any nearer." Like mother, like son, waiting was not my strong suit.

Too often, when I felt uneasy about what to do in any given situation, rather than sit in discomfort, I'd ask a friend or look to the internet to provide a quick answer I could act on.

Sitting in that awkward space between not knowing and not yet making a decision is where I've learned that the right answer will always make itself known. I just have to trust my gut to recognize it. But it's never immediate, and I find it to be annoyingly slower than I'd like. Hustling was my way of trying to outrun any uneasiness.

The answers to most of my problems aren't found when I'm in a hurry. I heard my voice echo as I taught myself while teaching my son: "Waiting is the better choice."

PART THREE

Curating
Making Space for What Fits

> To live is the rarest thing in the world. Most people exist, that is all.

— OSCAR WILDE

Breaking *Open*

RECENTLY READ AN ARTICLE THAT SAID 40 PERcent of people who retire get depressed, and it supported that gut feeling I've always had. I've watched plenty of people make plans to travel freely once they hit retirement age, only to find their health fade or find it difficult to abandon a mentality they had spent an entire lifetime building. The idea of retirement has always felt a little off.

As well-intended as financial advice may be, much of it is rooted in a scarcity mindset.

It tries to give us a sense of control in a life where we're not really in control. It scares us from coloring outside the lines and living creatively. Saving money, of course, can be a really healthy thing. It can help us in unforeseen circumstances, secure our independence, and keep us from financial hardship later in life. In these ways, being a saver feels right, wise even.

Shortly after college, when I began living on my own, I worried if my husband and I were putting away enough and clung ever so tightly to the little we had. The idea of donating to a cause would cross my mind, but that's all. What I spent my money on showed very clearly where my heart was. I should have been managing it, yet it felt like money was managing me.

I wanted a different approach to our finances, and still I didn't understand how to get there. When we jumped headfirst into creating our first business, it seemed like the natural starting point for getting out of the rat race. We spent months building up enough cushion for my husband to leave his corporate job and join me as cofounder, minimizing the risk despite limited funds and no insurance.

We went from a steady paycheck to watching our bank account dwindle month after month. When we finally got accepted into an accelerator, it felt like we had won the lottery. In some ways, we did. They offered us $25,000 for 6 percent of the company. The money was good, but the validation from people who saw potential in our business felt more like the real victory.

In a few weeks, we put our house up for rent, packed our bags, took our puggle, and moved into an apartment on Woodward Avenue in downtown Detroit. We cashed out our 401(k)s and savings, investing everything into our startup. As the months passed, the financial pressure intensified—nights filled with anxiety and days spent pitching to investors. Then, I got a call from my husband that would seal the fate of our startup. He had ruptured his Achilles' heel, ironically exposing our own. With only $10,000 in the bank and $11,000 needed for his surgery, the writing was on the wall.

We were broke.

We managed to negotiate our way out of our lease, packed up, and left Detroit with our tails between our legs. We retreated to my parents' house, grateful they welcomed us in, and set up camp in my childhood bedroom. I once read that it's not a lack of money that holds us back—it's the fear of losing what we have. Lying awake that first night back in my hometown, I felt the full weight of that truth.

Everything looked different from the bottom, clearer than I had imagined. At my worst, I had a husband who loved me, a family who offered help, and parents who took us in. We had no money; even so, we oddly had everything we needed. For months, I wrestled with what failure meant as a truthier truth began to surface: Just because the company failed didn't mean I was a failure.

Up until that point, an underlying fear had dictated the way I lived. Somewhere between a safe place to land and being surrounded by people who loved me, money lost its grip.

We weren't broke. We were broken open.

I thought the success of building a company would be what liberated me. When reality hit—our accounts drained, business in shambles, reputation muddied, and entirely reliant on others to pick up the pieces—I received a strange and unexpected gift: true freedom. Shutting down my business in front of everyone I knew really turned my idea of success upside down. For the first time, I started thinking about what it would mean to build a meaningful career—one that's about more than getting admiration or making money.

Being broken open like this made me realize I'd been "playing not to lose" for far too long. In basketball, that phrase describes when a team gets so focused on protecting their lead that they start playing timidly, afraid to make mistakes. But while they're preoccupied with holding on to what they have, they don't realize that this very mindset is costing them the game. Meanwhile, the other team—hungry, fearless, and with nothing to lose—gains momentum. And more often than not, they're the ones who end up winning.

When we play not to lose, we operate from fear—fear of failure, fear of losing what we've built, fear that without it, we won't be enough. We grip tightly to success, status, or approval, convincing ourselves that holding on is the only way to feel secure. But that grip, the desperation to keep control, only traps us. It blinds us to what's possible, keeping us small, stuck, and scared.

Entrepreneurship, or any creative pursuit, has shown me that clinging to something out of fear isn't living. It's surviving. And worse, it keeps me from ever knowing what else is out there.

I won't always win. But I refuse to live my life playing *not* to lose.

Getting Off
the Fence

A FTER MY FIRST STARTUP FAILED, I TOOK A "REAL" job at a local TV station in Cincinnati to get back on my feet. I had always liked the idea of working in news and media. Starting a blog wasn't pure happenstance. I used to get up early before high school to catch *Good Morning America*. Diane Sawyer, a fellow Midwesterner, even sent me an autographed photo after my mamaw mailed her a newspaper clipping where I was quoted saying that I wanted a job like hers.

My role was as close to being an entrepreneur inside a corporation as you could get. It was refreshing to work on

GETTING OFF THE FENCE

a product where funding wasn't a constant worry. I had two bosses: One sat over at the headquarters, and the other sat in the newsroom to oversee the execution of our initiative.

In my first big meeting, we were trying to pick a name for the subscription service. One boss was set on one name, and the other boss had a different favorite. Both of them, who happened to control my salary, slowly turned to me and asked, "What do you think?" Years of pitching to investors had shown me that I needed to wait it out to see what they wanted. I had learned my lesson in kindergarten. Here is where I played it cool, spouting off the pros and cons of each option. I thought I was being clever. Then one of my bosses looked me straight in the eye and said, "Erin, get off the fence." I felt exposed. They weren't looking for me to agree with them—they wanted my real opinion, even if it didn't line up with theirs. But there I was, holding back, not because I didn't have thoughts, but because I didn't want to stir the waters. The truth is, staying neutral had become my way of avoiding conflict. But the more I stayed quiet, the more I realized that playing it safe wasn't really safe at all—it was just another way of losing myself.

Every time I stayed quiet, I traded a little bit of my voice for someone else's. The moments when I had enough conviction to say what was on my mind were followed by an immediate call to a friend to get that extra reassurance.

Slowly, step by step, and with plenty of practice, I was learning to trust my own words. I saw it so clearly while watching my son learn to write. First, he had to figure out how to hold a pencil, then move on to tracing letters and numbers—his little hands unsteady, each stroke wobbly at first. I had completely forgotten about those early, shaky steps. How much work it takes to write. So why did I expect speaking freely to be any different? Like Roo, I was learning, even when it felt uncertain.

Looking *for* *the* Third Way

I'VE HEARD ABOUT THE NOTION OF BEING CHILD-like in Christianity. Or the beginner's mind, as it's called in Zen Buddhism. Both refer to wisdom about remaining open and limiting any preconceived bias.

Since I tended, at one time, to keep my distance from children, with their tendency for tantrums and their overall germiness, I struggled to understand. To me, acting more like a child wasn't the best advice.

Now as a parent, I can see a different side of things. My son is in constant discovery, where everything he experiences is new. He doesn't know what the best practices are or have a decade's experience to draw upon. There is no "normal" nor has he lived long enough to make up stories. There's an honest and unbiased way in which he interacts with the world.

His desire is insatiable, and he continually pushes boundaries to figure out if the sky's the limit. This mentality requires the occasional tweaking, demonstrated by the astronomical number of popsicles he'd consume given the chance, but I imagine even that would eventually normalize.

The mantra we hear is "the more you know." I think the opposite—"less is more"—might be better. In adulthood it's the stories I've told myself that keep me stuck. Letting logic cut me off from ever exploring. Exploring is where creativity finds its spark.

I call this "Handman Thinking."

Our first home was nestled on Handman Avenue, about three-quarters up a considerably large hill. I adored everything about this place, from its old-world charm and character to its stoop, akin to a Brooklyn brownstone and the so-called painted ladies, colorful houses that reminded me of a bit of San Francisco encapsulated in Cincinnati. We took the plunge and bought the house.

When we moved to Detroit to join the accelerator, we rented out our house on Handman. It was nothing short of a miracle that when the business folded, the rental income covered our mortgage, allowing us to keep the house. As our tenants wanted to find a place to buy, we started to regain our financial footing. I couldn't shake the feeling that moving back into our old house was a physical reflection of what we had been through. The house hadn't changed. We had.

I saw two options: go back to how things were or sell it.

One afternoon, sitting on a porch swing talking it over with my mom and husband, a third way revealed itself: renovation. Until that point, renovation had never even occurred to me. I had heard tales—horror stories—about people redoing their kitchens. Circa 2012, no one close to me had ever done anything like that. We didn't know a single contractor. *House Hunters* was my only point of reference.

I'm not sure what resonated more—breathing new life into a structure with a past or believing in its transformation when it was hard to see. Renovating was exactly what I needed that year. During the process I was restored right alongside our house. Childlike thinking didn't mean forgetting everything I knew. Logic delivers sound advice, but it was in remaining open that I found another way.

That, my friend, is where the third way revealed itself.

Stepping Back *to* Move Forward

MY HEART SKIPPED A BEAT WHEN THE EMAIL appeared in my inbox. Cursor hovering, I quickly surveyed the office to make sure no one was watching. I held my breath. Click. My eyes frantically scanned the email line by line until I found an official job offer from a startup. Not just any startup, but *Cladwell*, a fashion tech startup I didn't think would be possible to nail down without having to leave Cincinnati for New York. The same company I'd later end up running.

STEPPING BACK TO MOVE FORWARD

For three years, I'd been climbing upward in my corporate role. It didn't take much imagination to see how it could end: the fancy title, the big salary, and an office with a real door. It was a clearly defined path. All I had to do was stay on it. But I didn't want to stay on it. I had never wanted to be on it. I had taken the corporate job to get us back on our feet after the startup failed. When we were burnt out and our bank accounts depleted, it was the right call.

I tried to convince myself the corporate world was for me. After two years on "the path," I was restless. Tired of office politics. Drained by the tedious protocols. As scary as it was to try to go back to the startup world, it scared me far more to stay put. The answer was waiting in my inbox.

My heart sank when I saw the salary. It was a 40 percent pay cut.

I can't make less than I'm currently making. Won't that hurt my career?

It took me a minute to regain perspective. After shutting down my first startup, it felt like I had lost years in my career. Failure had clouded my judgment. In reality, that experience allowed me to bypass entry-level positions and jump straight into this corporate role. Taking a step back turned out to be the very thing that propelled me forward.

As my panic waned, I could see that this new role was what I had always wanted: fashion, tech, and in Cincinnati.

THE ROAD LESS WORN

It was an unlikely combination I wasn't convinced I would find. I thought the way to success resembled a straight line. Though looking back, it was clear that the biggest leaps in my career came from taking the detour.

That's how powerful the story in my head was. I had temporarily forgotten that stepping back wasn't a nice metaphor. It was my lived experience.

It had always been the way forward.

Choosing *a* Palette

E VERY NOW AND THEN, WE HAVE SLIDING DOOR moments that split our lives into two parts: before and after. The Sunday after I finished my first capsule was one of them. It was like waking up with a new pair of glasses—everything I thought I knew suddenly looked different, clearer, and less blurry.

Less clutter, more clarity.
Less impulsive, more intentional.
Less comparing, more creative.
Less chasing, more grounded.
Less was better, and I felt it.

I used to be indecisive, but now my closet was filled with only pieces I loved. It became easier to grab the first pair of jeans I saw, slip into an outfit, and get out the door. Mornings were no longer rushed.

Learning about color theory and exploring seasonal color palettes were only the beginning. Armed with this newfound understanding of how to curate a wardrobe that reflected me, I began to reevaluate past choices through a new lens, including my wedding dress. The soft ivory hue against my skin had me instantly saying yes to the dress. At the time, I couldn't fully articulate it. The choice of a soft white rather than a stark white was the very reason I felt more like myself.

We are naturally predisposed to seasonal colors: winter, autumn, spring, and summer. Our skin, hair, and eyes tell a story about us. Color reveals a unique distinction about who we are. To be clear, there's no rule book that says you can't venture out of wearing these shades. I never really paid attention to the colors I was buying, so my closet looked like a rainbow had thrown up. As I started to look a little closer, certain patterns began to stand out. The colors I naturally gravitated toward were the ones that matched my seasonal palette.

I started removing more and more colors that I bought but never wore. Curating based on what mixed and matched.

CHOOSING A PALETTE

I favored blues over purples and gravitated toward softer, more muted tones. Naming what I liked, or didn't, made what was once invisible visible.

From that moment, my approach to shopping transformed dramatically. I was no longer influenced by fleeting trends or the latest "color of the year." As a soft autumn, my color palette was well-defined, and my shopping rules were straightforward: buy only what I love and will wear over and over again.

My son does this better than anyone I know. The passion he exudes when he chooses his dinosaur shirt in the morning or his vitriol when I recommend a color he doesn't want near his skin is enlightening. Because of this, it always surprises me when I meet an adult who is indifferent about what they wear. As if they have no choice in what they put on before they step out the door.

When someone discovers that I work in fashion, their first reaction is often, "Don't judge me for what I'm wearing today." Or, my personal favorite, "My wife (or mom) does all my shopping."

It's no wonder the popularity of "uniforms" has taken off. I'm not talking about self-appointed outfits that can make mornings a breeze. I'm talking about the signature looks of cultural icons like Steve Jobs, Mark Zuckerberg, or Richard Branson. Minimalism for efficiency's sake. The idea is appealing: less comparison, fewer decisions, more time for what truly matters. Even monks have long embraced this philosophy.

Every time I stumble upon another article praising the idea of uniforms, I can't help but wonder if efficiency is a mask—an easy way to avoid the harder questions. It feels like adulting 101—trading joy for practicality and patting ourselves on the back for being so smart. It doesn't have to be either/or. I've learned you can have both.

Simplifying my wardrobe has shown me that getting dressed doesn't have to be a daily struggle—it can be effortless, even enjoyable. A capsule wardrobe functions like a well-designed uniform, cutting through the chaos of decision fatigue and replacing it with ease. But its real magic is in what it unlocks: creativity. When we strip away the excess and keep only what we love, every outfit becomes a piece of who we are—without hesitation. Instead of feeling limited, bored, and confined by wearing the same thing over and over, we feel liberated.

My son reminded me that getting dressed each day isn't just about being seen—it's a choice. In a world that constantly pushes us to conform, the simple act of choosing what to wear can be a subtle, unspoken rebellion. We live in an age obsessed with big transformations, yet for me, it was the small, seemingly insignificant choices—gravitating

CHOOSING A PALETTE

toward certain colors, repeating outfits I loved—where I began to find my way back to who I am.

I let go of the need to justify my preferences and started trusting that loving something was reason enough. And somewhere in those everyday decisions I stopped second-guessing, and a steadier version of myself began to take shape.

Questioning Happily Ever After

'M A SUCKER FOR FAIRY TALES. ALWAYS HAVE BEEN. Show me the movie with the girl struggling to figure out who she is, only to discover herself (and her dreamy husband), and I'll watch it nine times. Give me the woman who has to prove herself to get the dream job, and I'll watch it ten times.

The issue with happily ever after, in movies or real life, is that it never paints the whole picture. Our messy humanness sits right out of frame.

QUESTIONING HAPPILY EVER AFTER

I heard a story about how, when the cameras stopped rolling during *The Oprah Winfrey Show*, she regularly asked her audience, "What do you really want in life?" The most resounding and common answer was, "I want to be happy."

It's not surprising. We've all heard it or even said it out loud. Like any good interviewer, Oprah probed. She followed up with a simple question: "What does happiness look like for you?"

Murmuring and squirming in their seats, people would fumble through their vague answers—something about their kids, health, or income—never fully able to articulate or confidently define this so-called happiness.

It's not that people were lying, but they weren't telling the whole truth, either. Here's how I think about it. It's like wearing a designer jacket over old, torn jeans—then only showing the jacket in your Instagram post. You're not lying about wearing the jacket, but you're not revealing the entirety of your outfit. Half-truths work the same way. You share some truth while conveniently leaving out other parts to shape how people see you.

We choose which truths to share and which to hide, crafting a narrative that serves a specific purpose, much like curating an image or style.

"The pursuit of happiness" is practically ingrained in our American psyche. According to Oprah's audience, we aim our entire lives at this goal without even defining what "happiness" actually means to us.

I was no different. Believing happiness was the goal made every setback feel paralyzing—like I was somehow getting life wrong, desperate to fast-forward through the hard parts. But the more I lived, the more I came to see that the messy middle—the struggles, the questions, the uncertainty—is where real growth happens.

And if happiness is the only thing we hope to have, there's a good chance we'll bail before we ever get to the good stuff.

Preparing *to* Fly

With sand between my toes, sweat drops pooling along my hairline, and the ocean waves breaking at my feet, I broke.

It had been an incredibly difficult two years. After our business went bust, I was left picking up the pieces of the company and the broken partnership that left me with scars. Trying to put everything back together during a global pandemic was like working on a two-thousand-piece puzzle with no reference image for how it all fit together. At times, I was certain it wasn't going to work out.

But that day, on the beach, I saw the path forward.

A young seagull with the tiniest of feet took off running in a full sprint across the sand. Then, inches from my chair, the bird lifted into the air with absolute ease.

It wasn't that I'd never seen a seagull fly. It was that I'd never paid attention to what happens right before its flight. The transition, I had missed all these years.

With sunlight beaming on my face and salt in the air, I had a breakthrough.

To go from standing to flying in an instant is nearly impossible. Unnatural, even. The seagull needed space. Just as I did. I had been running—full sprint—unaware of the abundance of grace that lives in the transition. The space between point A (the new Cladwell CEO) and point B (coming into my own) was the time I needed to heal, find my footing, and aim for something new.

The beach vacation ended. On the way home, I knew deep down that I was prepared to lift off.

Change was coming.

Finding *Your* People

IT SEEMED UNREMARKABLE FROM THE OUTSIDE. Another graduate is leaving for college. For me, it was a quiet rebellion. It wasn't that I wanted to leave where I grew up. I knew that I needed to get out.

I walked into my freshman dorm to meet my new roommate and teammate, Katie. She grew up in a small town that mirrored my own. Only hers was settled in the South, where they said things like "fixin'" and "y'all." We quickly bonded over how sports had turned us into the Golden Girls. Laughing about how loud our bones cracked and how we both had to have custom-made orthopedic insoles. In a year, Katie restored my view of friendship—nights spent in our bunks binge-watching TLC. College was everything I had hoped it would be: a breath of fresh air where competition and jealousy weren't prerequisites for friendship. Instead of viewing her or my success as a threat, we celebrated and supported each other's accomplishments. Miles away from home, I found friendship again.

As I navigated my freshman year, I took to heart my sister's clear directive. She's not one to dish out advice, so when she does, I listen: "Don't get into a relationship your first year of college. Have fun and enjoy your freedom."

I often wondered if her words came from her own experience or perhaps they were protecting me from our grandparents' belief that going to college was a matter of pursuing our "M.R.S. Degree." Either way, I had every intention of following her wise words. That is, until I met him.

"Do you know how much a polar bear weighs?"

"No," I responded back.

"Enough to break the ice. Hi, I'm Colin."

The gesture was ridiculous and beyond cheesy, and yet I couldn't resist. It took me all of one day on campus to forget any sisterly wisdom. He was on the men's basketball team. I was on the women's. Both of us hailed from the Midwest. His upbringing was in Cincinnati, surrounded by busy streets and chain restaurants. I grew up between corn fields and soybeans. His version of chili was poured over spaghetti. Mine had spaghetti in it. His brain worked like an engineer. Mine was more like an artist. He lived without worries. I gathered all of them. Different. Yet so much alike. It was *Love & Basketball* but the whiter, way less cool version.

We were young with ambition. We spent our days dreaming, wanting to pave our way. We wondered who lived in those big homes with nice neighborhoods. What were their jobs? How might we become them?

If we're lucky, we have a few people in our lives like Colin and Katie.

Those who don't add to our story but remind us to tell our own.

Breaking *the* Rules

There's a phrase in business: "the best leaders work themselves out of a job."

For years, I followed this principle, thinking the right way to run a business was to hire people who were smarter than me. I worked myself out of a company I had no plans to ever leave. It took me far too long to realize that this advice was flawed.

I'm not saying that hiring smart people is a bad idea. Or that building up your team to fill gaps as you take on new responsibilities isn't worth your time. If you like "the work," hear me when I say this: Never getting to do it is a surefire path to self-destruction.

For years, I let stories like these dictate my role as a "good CEO" rather than trusting my ability to lead in my own way.

It pigeonholed me into one position: "management." I delegated responsibilities so I could work on the business, not in it, keeping the ship steady in case I ever decided to walk away. It wasn't that I wanted to reject success, but I needed to redefine it. I had spent so much time trying to do things "the right way" that I hadn't stopped to ask whether that way worked for me. Maybe success wasn't about stepping back from the work I loved, but about staying close to what energized me. Maybe leadership didn't have to mean managing from a distance, but rather, leading by doing.

It wasn't until I asked, "Why isn't this fun anymore?" that I let myself explore what I would do if I left. All my ideas sounded eerily similar to my current job when it finally clicked. I had outsourced the things that piqued my interest in the name of passivity: all the fun parts that spurred my creativity.

For many people, building a business is an act of creating. We don't have to move on to the next one to find interesting work. Sometimes, we need a subtle reminder that if something doesn't feel right, we have the ability to change it.

It's similar to starting a new book only to realize you don't have to finish it before reading the next. These little spoken or unspoken rules can be broken. Being a founder never barred me from creating or designing any more than a restaurateur has to stop cooking or a chief technology officer has to stop coding. Said like that, it almost seems silly.

Work tends to get a bad rap, and it's easy to fall into the mindset of trying to "work ourselves out of a job." But the best kind of work—the kind that fills us up—isn't about escaping it. It's about finding joy in the process of creating, of building something we care about. When I leaned into what I loved, work wasn't just something to get through—it became life-giving, soul-filling, and something I was made to do.

If you are eager to leave a job only to want a similar one, ask yourself, "What do I miss creating?"

Finding myself as a CEO wasn't about climbing some ladder—it was about finding my way back to the work that brought me life.

Because the best leaders? They actually like their jobs.

PART FOUR

Capsule Living
Creating Your Own Way

> The things that we love tell us what we are.

—THOMAS AQUINAS

Exploration

IMAGINE YOU'VE FINALLY CLEANED OUT YOUR closet, removed all the excess, and then stepped back. You take a look, seeing the space in between the hangers, and you exhale. It doesn't end here. You know tomorrow you'll have to get dressed. That's where living with a capsule wardrobe starts. That's where the real work begins.

Like each item, each story I had held on to had been laid out in front of me, and while this new clarity was freeing, I found myself at a loss about what to do next.

What now? There were no more piles to sort through, no immediate decisions demanding my attention. The purpose of the cleanout was clear—to simplify, to create space. Once that space was made, the real exploration began. There were no preset milestones or stories I had to follow in order to live my best life. That was kind of the whole point. It was quiet.

There was an uneasiness at first. I wasn't practiced at listening to the kindest, most genuine voice inside me. Gradually, though, I began trusting in its wisdom.

My mom used to tell me a story about how my papaw coached. He was known for sitting calmly on the sidelines while most coaches paced along the bench yelling at their players. Not him. His theory was simple: If players hadn't learned it in practice, they certainly wouldn't learn it in the middle of a game. Practice is where we hone our craft so that we're free to play when we set foot on the court.

It wasn't that long ago that I used to think freedom was buying whatever I wanted whenever I wanted. But liberation has come in having tried and true practices, seasonal rhythms, and daily routines. In *The Creative Act*, Rick Rubin says, "It is often the case that the more set in your regimen, the more freedom you have within that structure to express yourself."

The capsule wardrobe wasn't confining—it freed me to be myself. By choosing outfits I loved and wearing them often, no matter what anyone else thought, I solidified my sense of identity. I became confident in my style, able to steer clear of the fleeting trends pushed by influencers season after season.

The same goes for how I choose to live each day. The noise, the pressure, the never-ending to-do lists that once ran my life don't have the same hold on me anymore. Instead, I've held on to a few essentials—the habits, rhythms, and values that truly make life better. These are the things that ground me and bring clarity when everything else feels overwhelming.

In the next few sections, I'll share what remained beneath the clutter—what I've kept and what I'm building my life around.

Surrender

I THOUGHT I'D LOST THE COMPANY, AND I BEGAN spiraling, like one does when they don't have a clue what they are going to do next. There was no backup job or plan B—everything I had was invested in this. It felt like the end.

Then, a new possibility began to come to light: There was a chance to buy what remained of the company. I was supposed to be this empowered millennial woman, fully capable of running her own business. In truth, I was terrified. Everything about the business screamed "run for the hills"—messy code, angry customers, no team, and an unclear business model. To be frank, it was a dumpster fire. I had done the mental math on our chances of

SURRENDER

reviving it, and it didn't look promising. If there was ever a time to bail, wipe my hands clean, and start over in my career, this was it.

Yet part of me saw its potential. I was on the brink of sitting in the driver's seat for once. Doubts were the only thing holding me back. What if I can't fix it? What if it fails? What if I can't handle the pressure?

I had to move beyond the doubts.

To be clear, I realize that the risk of failing isn't just the risk of being inconvenienced—for many of us, it can mean a literal place out on the streets. It wasn't that long ago that I found myself cooped up in my childhood room. So I'm not here to naively tell you that no matter the circumstance, starting something new is always worth the risk.

But I knew my instinct was to hold on too tightly, determined to make it work at all costs. Buying the company didn't appeal to me if it meant staying stuck in my usual patterns of thinking. So, I loosened my grip and made peace with the uncertainty. There was no guarantee of success or failure, but I decided to take the leap anyway.

I was ready to take on the role of CEO, come what may.

Playing *Another* Game

WHEN I STARTED MY FIRST BUSINESS, I HAD NO idea what I was doing. Wracked with insecurities and imposter syndrome, I attended meetups and events and joined the startup ecosystem, which put me in the presence of people with answers—predominantly men in positions of power.

What began as a desire to meet and learn from the startup community quickly became a chase for validation. This wasn't the first time I had tried to prove I could hang with the boys.

PLAYING ANOTHER GAME

Morristown, Indiana. Spring of '92. Second grade. Recess was in session, and Corey, the class-crowned basketball champ, challenged me to a one-on-one game. While some kids headed for the swings, many more gathered around the cracked, black pavement to watch. Knee socks were pulled high, and my ponytail was even higher. I stood tall in my usual tomboy attire. Pressure bubbling up inside, I stepped out on the court. We checked the ball at the top of the key and the game began. I played it hard.

With my sweet victory came bragging rights, a new title, and the stress of upholding it.

I've found startup culture to be disturbingly similar to my second-grade playground. Although I wasn't afraid to step onto the court, having to prove myself repeatedly was exhausting. A few years into my startup journey, it was clear that raising capital was the name of the game. With limited places to secure funding, the gatekeepers—mostly older men—held all the power. Whoever could convince those gatekeepers they were most worthy won the cash.

So I played the game and played it hard. I participated in countless pitch competitions and demo days, talked at length with *Shark Tank* producers, and was featured in *TechCrunch* articles and on *Good Morning America*, touting the latest raise or greatest feature.

After a decade of being a female founder in a male-dominated tech industry, I finally realized there is no winning in business. Proving myself in a game that can't be won gives me a brief moment of satisfaction before that feeling of fulfillment slips away.

I've moved from doubting myself to trusting my gut. It didn't happen overnight. It took practice, a lot of it. Along the way, titles and bragging rights lost their appeal.

From the outside, it might look like I've lost my competitive edge. But it hasn't disappeared—it's evolved. I no longer waste energy attempting to prove my worth to people who were never going to see it in the first place. The game I'm playing is different now. It's one that will last.

Creating *Space*

I'T'S MONDAY MORNING, 8:30 A.M. THE SUN IS MAK-
ing its first appearance for the day. I'm down a single cup
of coffee when the anxiety stirs within. I take a deep breath
and push the feelings aside. Sipping the second cup of coffee is easy, but the walk to my desk is not. Panic awaits.

At 9:00 a.m., I had already fallen behind. The to-do list, the pressure to do more, my inner dialogue spiraling.

You're behind.

How is the launch going to work if we don't have a plan?

So much to do. Not enough time.

I'm going to miss my chance.

Like the rush of adrenaline when the starting gun fires at a track meet, I lunge off the starting block into a full sprint—action in the form of Slack messages, urgent meetings, and a stream of aggressive questions directed at my team. My intentions are good. I want the business to succeed and the team to reach its full potential. Healthy moves rarely come after a string of anxious thoughts.

My kind of anxiety looks like overperforming, something coaches and bosses often praised. In this mode, I can make quick, big decisions and give team directives like a military general. Part of my innate superpower is to go and to go fast. It's also my kryptonite. For a few militant Monday morning moments, I trick myself into thinking this is the best version of me.

Spoiler alert...it's not.

It became clear that, like my closet, I had crammed my life with endless tasks and constant proof of value. I've been sorting through each part wondering how I got so turned around, uncovering the root of each story, piece by piece. I began by applying the principles of capsule wardrobing to my life. Then, I started outlining what "a better way" of living could look like.

- **Identity:** Who I aspire to be.
- **What I Love:** Accepting who I am.

- What I Don't Love: Letting go of who I no longer aim to become.
- What I Value: Keeping only what is beautiful, useful, or valuable to my life.
- Setting Boundaries: Sitting in the discomfort of disappointing others rather than disappointing myself.
- Living Free: Creating rhythms where what I do matches my core beliefs.

I've started some new habits on Mondays, too. Instead of diving into Slack and Gmail first thing, I seek beauty and inspiration. Maybe I'll go for a walk to shake off the anxious energy, or I might start the day with a book to calm my mind. It might go against the whole "early bird gets the worm" idea, but this routine keeps me grounded. It makes me a better person to be around and, in the long run, more productive.

I've learned that creating space between my anxiety and my actions changes everything. It reminds me that panic isn't who I am—it's just an old story that used to take the wheel. Now, I see Mondays differently. They're my built-in reset button, a chance to pause and ask myself: What's driving me this week? Is it fear? Do I need space?

Trusting *Yourself*

Time and again, I've made the same mistake: I place trust in others more than myself, believing they possess something that I don't have.

This pattern comes to light when I'm in a hurry, searching for a quick solution. I try to keep the pace, taking other people's advice or outsourcing tasks so as not to lose any time. After all, isn't that what we're taught? That the answers lie outside of us? That someone else—an expert, a mentor, a success story—must have figured it out already?

One of the hardest parts of rewriting my own narrative has been knowing when to take advice and when to trust my own instincts. It's rarely clear-cut—especially when the wisdom comes from an authority figure or is packaged as a success story that worked for someone else. And it's even harder when the voices offering advice belong to the people we love. But just like cleaning out my closet, I've had to learn that not every opinion deserves a place in my life. Some stories fit. Some don't. The real work is in deciding what to keep—clearing enough space to let my own voice come through.

At the core of a capsule wardrobe is the practice of slowing down to listen to ourselves. And at the core of my life's work is learning to trust myself as deeply as I've been taught to trust others.

Choosing Satisfaction

LISTENING TO MYSELF IS ONE THING—ACTING ON it is another. Because at the core of trust is choice. The choice to believe that what I already have is enough. The choice to stop chasing and start being.

I came across the Japanese term *chisoku*, which can be translated to simply "be satisfied." I couldn't help but wonder what the American version was.

Maybe, "There is always more"?

The internet has given us opportunities our parents' generation couldn't begin to fathom—a way to make a living without ever leaving our home or even physically

CHOOSING SATISFACTION

making something. We have access to more money, more clothes, more fame, and more followers than ever before. The cognitive dissonance between more access and our collective mental state has me wondering whether we've lost all notion of what it means to "be satisfied."

Capitalism touts that having a lot of choices equals freedom. The moment those choices are taken away, well, we're obviously on a slippery slope to communism. America in a nutshell.

We experience a paradox of choice, thinking, "I have too many clothes and nothing to wear," while staring at an overstuffed closet. Even when we are free to choose, it doesn't mean we have the ability. Our closets show how if we don't set our standards, the world will happily set them for us. And if we follow the world's standard for how much we "should have," we will never have enough. We will never truly feel *chisoku*.

Wanting a new thing isn't bad. Evolving or changing it up is natural. I love reinventing my seasonal style or pursuing a new dream. There are times when, deep down in my bones, I feel a panic of sorts that my "wanting" is driven by something other than me entirely. I'll slip into the "there's always more" trap—not doing enough, working enough, having enough, being enough. There will always be more clothes I can buy, more capital I can go after, and more to-dos I can check off my list. More. More. More. Freedom exists in the space where I've finally chosen what's *enough* for me.

In the past, I thought *feeling enough* meant settling. Like if I wasn't always pushing for more, I was somehow giving up. But *chisoku* isn't about quitting on dreams, it's about accepting that real fulfillment isn't in the chase. It's in choosing what actually matters and letting that be enough.

It felt uneasy seeing items I could buy, ideas I could turn into businesses, and followers I could have pass me by. Real freedom isn't in having unlimited choices. It's in knowing when I already have what I need.

Mending

After a delightful dinner downtown, I was heading back to my car, soaking in the evening, when I spotted my old cofounder across the street. I thought I had moved past our old ties, but suddenly, I found myself walking a little faster and looking down. It was as if I was a two-year-old, thinking if I didn't see him, then he couldn't see me.

I opened the door and jumped in the car, hoping the windows were dark enough I couldn't be seen. No matter how much work I had done to heal the scars, I was reminded that remnants still remained.

There are pain points that, when scraped in an unexpected moment, can transport me back to an era I so desperately tried to move on from. For a long time, I thought forgiveness meant that negative feelings would never resurface. That, somehow, forgiving would remove my humanness. A dinner shop run-in proved otherwise.

Emotions came flooding back, and a guilt-ridden meltdown followed close behind.

This again, really?

Have I done forgiveness all wrong?

I thought I was over it.

Haven't I moved on by now?

As it turns out, forgiveness isn't magic, and I'm not a wizard. Rather, it's a practice for us mere mortals.

While I've spoken openly about the failure of my first startup and friendships that fell apart, there are many other setbacks I haven't shared, fearing others' judgment. I worry I'm not the only one who feels pressure to curate and perform, making sure our story is polished and bright, hiding away any flaws.

In Japan, there's an art form called *kintsugi*, where broken pottery is repaired with gold, symbolizing that our pain can be transformed into something beautiful. I've come to see that facing the hard stuff head-on, whether it's navigating through clutter or addressing what's broken, is the only path to uncovering the good stuff.

The art of *kintsugi* beautifully illustrates that the path to wholeness is paved with mending. When emotions bubble up, they don't erase the progress we've made; rather, they invite us back to the healing practice of forgiveness.

While time alone may not heal, practice could very well be the gold that binds us back together.

Loosening *the* Grip

I WOKE UP ON A COLD AND GLOOMY SATURDAY morning with big plans sketched out in my mind.

I had spent the night before lying in bed, dreaming about making the morning less chaotic and more peaceful for my son and I while my husband played pickleball. I'm not one to enjoy playing pretend while being cooped up in the house, so I needed an alternative option, and fast—something that would keep my energy high and my sanity higher.

Nothing extravagant, but leaving the house would ensure I would be my best self. The plans had been set: head down to the Meat Market to grab some breakfast tacos, then swing by our local coffee shop for a kid's milk and a vanilla latte, followed by a quick stroll over to the public library to return his books and grab some new ones to entertain us for the rest of the day.

My son had a different idea.

Before we could take off his pajamas and put on real clothes, a dance party broke out in front of the mirror. Then, a few toy dinosaurs joined in and it turned out they needed a good bathing in the shower.

The longer he played, the more I could feel the tension rising up within me. Shoulders and neck tightening, my mind in an endless loop of all the ways we were already behind schedule. Then, it hit me. There was no "schedule" when I was the one who created it.

He happily played alone in the shower, and I seemingly had time to myself. I had let an image in my head of what our day should be ruin what otherwise was a pleasant morning. This Saturday was insignificant, yet it stirred a feeling, adjusting far more than my expectations.

I started thinking about control. And control, I do. A hard "J" in the Myers-Briggs, I can spend hours fixating on plans, creating a laundry list of to-dos, and checking off each one without any room for happenstance. This approach often sucks the joy out of these so-called fun activities.

THE ROAD LESS WORN

Here's the thing about tension: It can't exist if it's not being pulled between what is and what could be. When we loosen our grip on our invented plans—the expectations we set—we begin to experience all the beautiful ways life simply unfolds. Beauty that we couldn't have otherwise seen.

Space can be uncomfortable because it challenges us to take a long, hard look at our best-laid plans and determine whether what we're holding on to is the root of our pain. For me, it was something as simple and obvious as a Saturday morning with my son. Holding on to expectations of what could have been was the difference between whether or not I enjoyed a day with him.

He, on the other hand, was perfectly content.

Wielding *Our* Strength

Only 2 percent of the garment workers, who are mostly women, earn enough to support their basic needs. At the same time, women make up 84 percent of the influencers on Instagram, often promoting the very brands these workers produce for. This sharp contrast reveals an opportunity: Women have the potential to address and influence the profound disparities affecting other women around the world.

Women dominate consumer decisions, making 80 percent of them. If we decided to stop supporting companies that don't share our values tomorrow, we could fundamentally shake up business models across the nation. We could persuade their corporate leaders and governments to rethink their practices, potentially leading to more ethical and sustainable operations and, ultimately, fairer wages.

There is a psychological phenomenon in Buddhism called "near enemies." I believe this is one of the main reasons we get pulled into these cultural currents quicker than ever. An article in *The Guardian* explains it as follows:

> For every desirable habit or state of mind, there's a "far enemy," which is its obvious antithesis. Thus hatred, it won't surprise you to learn, is the far enemy of love. Near enemies, on the other hand, are much sneakier and harder to spot, because they so closely resemble the thing they're the enemy of. Needy, possessive codependency can look and feel a lot like love, when really it corrodes it.

Look no further than recycling plastics as an example. As NPR reported in their investigative series:

> Starting in the late 1980s, the plastics industry spent tens of millions of dollars promoting recycling through ads, recycling projects and public relations, telling people plastic could be and should be recycled.

Their own internal records dating back to the 1970s show that industry officials long knew that recycling plastic on a large scale was unlikely to ever be economically viable.

The industry promoted recycling to keep plastic bans at bay.

The plastic industry grasped a fundamental human truth: Once we think we're doing good, we tend to stop searching for better ways to make a difference. Why keep searching if we believe we're already doing enough? But we were misled.

Similar to how the plastics industry has historically championed recycling despite knowing the economic reality on a large scale, the fashion industry now employs similar "greenwashing" tactics. It pays influencers to wear sustainably made clothes designed intentionally to bypass the heart of the issue—our shopping habits. It ignores the staggering amount of clothing consumed year after year.

I was reading a piece in the *Harvard Business Review* that talked about how some of the best ideas can come from people who aren't wrapped up in the norms of a particular industry. These are the people who bring fresh, new perspectives simply because they're not bogged down by the usual way of doing things.

Fitting the mold of strong, independent women breaking barriers sounds admirable—like those mastering the Instagram game, building brands, and cashing in. But these days, I'm after something deeper—the kind of earth-shaking change that comes from those willing to step off the beaten path entirely, to leave the algorithm behind and create a successful life on their own terms.

Claiming *Space*

IN 1967, LONG BEFORE I WAS BORN, KATHRINE Switzer officially became the first woman to run the Boston Marathon. Until then, the Boston Marathon was a male-only event, and women were prohibited from participating. Let that sink in for a minute. Running, a natural human instinct, was not permitted for women, at least "officially."

She quietly entered the race under the name "K.V. Switzer." Not making it obvious she was a female allowed her to slip through the cracks undetected. As she was running, the word got out when race official Jock Semple, who was following the rules, tried to stop her. In a forceful act, he attempted to physically remove Switzer from the course. Switzer's boyfriend at the time, Thomas Miller, who was running with her, pushed Semple away—blocking him so she could continue and finish the marathon.

If you haven't seen the photo of the incident, stop reading here and Google it. It paints a vivid picture of how women were perceived a generation ago. I still remember the first time I heard this story, seated in the back of a mahogany-paneled college classroom, looking up at a picture projected on the screen. My mind was blown.

Like Kathrine, I've felt torn between two roles more than once. Maybe you've felt this, too, in your career or role at home. It feels like ancient history, but it wasn't that long ago when women were sidelined. To put this into perspective, my mom was part of the first formally organized girls' basketball team at my high school. It wasn't as long ago as it seems.

Kathrine entered the race to prove that she, like anyone else, could complete a marathon. She didn't set out that day to challenge gender norms or make a political statement. She ran for the same reason I've now come to see so clearly: because she could.

Decluttering my clothes, then my life, was never about proving a point. It was about taking back what was already mine. The hardest part of doing something without permission isn't the act itself. It's trusting, deep down, that you belong there in the first place.

She ran because she knew the space was hers.

And now, so do I.

Making *It* Personal

EVERY TIME I HEAR THE WORDS, "IT'S BUSINESS. It's not personal," I feel the need to take a shower. Sure, the intent behind the phrase may be innocent enough. Though when a family-owned bookshop goes under because all their customers flocked to the big-box bookstore around the corner, try telling them, "It's just business." Business is always personal simply because we're human.

My experience with my startups has made this evident, and saying some pithy phrase doesn't make it any less so.

Making it personal doesn't mean being fragile. The way

MAKING IT PERSONAL

we show up in our work, our relationships, and our decisions matters. It's not about taking every criticism to heart but about leading with integrity. Even the most intellectual and logical thinkers are emotional beings driven by the stories they tell themselves. While the ups and downs of running a business may be out of our control, we always have a choice in how dignified we are to others. Hard decisions impact real humans with feelings, responsibilities, and families. As Meg Ryan states in *You've Got Mail*, "It's personal to me."

We're humans first. As soon as I'm out of the shower, I'd like to adjust this story.

Business is personal.

Bearing *Fruit*

IN THE WORLD OF BUSINESS, THERE'S A SAYING that's heard across boardrooms and offices: "If you're not growing, you're dying."

At face value, it sounds like if we're not making something bigger, we're sliding into oblivion. This story has caused me to hustle for my worth more than I care to admit. These stories we grew up with aren't wrong. They have a sliver of the truth. As we age, we get to fill in the rest. We get to tell the whole story.

For years, I believed growth was about scale—about doing more, reaching more, earning more. But real growth, the kind that actually lasts, has to do with depth. It's knowing what to pour into and what to let go.

Growth in my business has felt elusive at times, especially compared to the latest viral sensation. I've dabbled in it all, trying to make growth take off.

Press coverage? I've given it a go.

Outfits of the day videos? Call me the next influencer.

And paid ads? My bank statement would prefer we don't delve into that.

But take a look at how nature does growth; it's nothing like this. Consider an apple tree, for instance. It bides its time, waiting years before bearing its first fruit. It can't sprout more branches or force itself to produce apples out of season. We don't criticize it when it stops growing taller, nor do we expect it to curl over and die when it's reached its full height. Real growth, the kind that truly matters, is about deepening our roots and creating a space where we, and those around us, can flourish.

Reflecting on the growth I had pictured in my twenties, I realize it sounds closer to the greed Dr. Seuss talked about in *The Lorax*. The idea of "biggering," as he put it, could really impact both ourselves and the world we live in.

Our language matters. It's part of how our culture is brought to life. The way we talk about our projects and businesses sounds more like we're managing a hostage situation rather than a company.

"Execute."

"Hustle harder."

"Rise and grind."

"24/7."

What if we talked about our businesses or creative projects not as machinery to be optimized but as gardens to be cultivated?

"If you're not growing, you're dying." It's a catchy phrase. A more nuanced truth I've come to understand is this: Growth isn't always visible on the surface. Often, it's where the roots are being laid.

Focusing *on* *the* Essentials

I HAVE TO BE CAREFUL WITH HOW HARD I WORK, making sure I'm not just using it as a way to trick myself into thinking I can control the outcome. The truth is, I'm learning to trust that things will unfold as they're meant to. Not perfectly, by any means, but by focusing on small, intentional changes that feel right for me.

1. **Digital Sabbath:** I set aside one day a week when I don't check email, Slack, or social media. This gives me mental space to hear my thoughts without scrolling through those of others.

2. Silence Notifications: I used to feel constantly behind. I quickly realized that being bombarded at all hours of the day wasn't helping. I silence all work-related notifications from my phone. Now, I check my email, Slack, or social media only at certain points throughout the day to make sure I prioritize my work rather than my work prioritizing me.

3. Mindful Shopping: I make a short list of items I'd like to add after curating my wardrobe each season. It's a simple way of being intentional in my shopping habits.

4. Daily Walks: I'm a better human if I walk, period. Put me on the beach somewhere, and I'm an even better human there. I don't know if it's being in nature or moving around, but walking is the antidote to any bad day.

5. Morning Reading: Reading in the morning has become a rhythm as valued as my cup of coffee. Some days, it's only a page. Sometimes, it is all it takes to help move my mind in a new direction, giving me a little perspective.

Each practice keeps me honest, because I've learned: If we don't choose our path, someone else will.

Going *Our* Way

LEARNING TO SAY WHAT I ACTUALLY FEEL ON THE inside has taken some time.

A few weeks ago, my husband and I told our extended family we wouldn't be joining them on a trip. I'm a nervous flier, and the thought of a seven-hour flight with a young kid—plus the detailed planning required for a large group to stay in the jungle—felt overwhelming. For a lot of people, that kind of adventure sounds incredible. For me, it was anxiety-ridden.

It took everything in me to say, "Go on without us on this one."

Weeks later, over coffee, a friend mentioned that her whole family—five kids and a husband—were heading to Singapore for spring break. It sounded exactly like her—adventurous, fearless, totally unbothered by logistics.

The moment she said it, doubt crept in. If she can do it with five kids, shouldn't I be able to handle it with one? Am I making a mistake? Should I change my mind?

I recognized the familiar pattern immediately. I have a habit of forcing other people's definitions of a good time or a good life onto my own. Whether it's tweaking my morning routine because someone swears "morning people are more successful" or rethinking how much funding my business should secure after reading a single article, I try to fit a square peg into a round hole—because someone else said it was good.

It's taken me years to unlearn this: Just because I can do something, doesn't mean I should.

Playing *for* Joy

O N AN ALMOST-SUMMER DAY, AS PERFECT AS they come in Cincinnati in early June, I reveled in the sheer joy of 78 degrees without a hint of humidity. This was my perfect temperature.

Lacing up my shoes, I walked down my driveway, setting off on my usual walking route. Straight across from my house, the community water tower stands tall beside a basketball court, the site of regular pickup games in the evenings, frequented by the younger neighborhood boys and their friends.

Walking on the sidewalk, I approached the stretch to my next crossing, where the road curved ever so slightly. As I continued walking along, I passed by a young girl. I was so engrossed in my favorite podcast that it took me a moment to truly see her.

I felt like I had happened on the Ghost of Christmas Past—or rather, a reflection of my own. She appeared to be around ten, her dirty blond hair tied back in a low ponytail, dressed in mesh shorts and a T-shirt. She wore a black sweatband around her head and dribbled a basketball. As we were about to cross paths, she lifted her eyes, looking directly at me, smiling as though we knew each other.

I was taken aback.

A few more steps past her, I found myself doing a double take, looking again, questioning my state of mind. Had I conjured her up, or was she really there?

Our neighborhood is not large, and my daily walks have familiarized me with most of the people who live nearby. Yet, never before had I encountered a girl in full tomboy attire, with a sweatband mirroring the image of my ten-year-old self. For the next mile, my mind wandered to the advice career coaches and psychologists often give when we feel lost: remember what you loved before you felt the need to become someone.

I'm not sure what I saw, but I do know this—after a long week, it was exactly the reminder I needed of who I was before the world got a hold of me.

I was that little girl who walked toward the nearest court, ponytail bobbing, mesh shorts intact, New Balance shoes laced up, and the basketball nestled in my right hand. I wasn't concerned about proving anything.

I played for the simple joy of it.

Accepting *Who* We Are

There he was, knees tucked up to his chest. Lucky Charms on one side, and two worn-out blankies on the other. My little Roo. I sat admiring him from the other couch, coffee in hand, suddenly compelled to ask him, "What do you want to be when you grow up?" He looked me straight in the eye without hesitation: "I want to be Rooney!"

"Right!" I smiled. "Of course!"

Why would it occur to him that he should be anyone but himself? He didn't know how wise he was. When I playfully tease, "Let's go, Fred!" he'll counter with, "I'm not Fred, I'm Rooney!" As if he must remind me who he is.

To watch him is to remember that I didn't come into this world striving to be anything other than who I was. Somewhere along the way (clearly after age three), I became aware of what others thought of me. I was taught, in the smallest of moments, making adjustments over time, that doing what others approved of would win them over.

The older I get, the more I realize that living a meaningful life means returning to what I knew when I was young. Rooney holds the wisdom I've forgotten.

Growing up isn't so much about "becoming somebody" as it is about accepting who we are and retracing our steps back to what's been buried beneath the clutter.

Feeling *Whole*

T HE WORD "ALONE" WAS THE WORD I KEPT COMING back to when writing how this new way of living felt. It was throwing me off. Alone had always seemed like a scary word. After all, we know there's safety in numbers—less risk when we follow the pack. Watch any clip on *National Geographic* to see this phenomenon play out. Being alone meant being the character you don't want to be in the movies or the older lady eating at the corner booth in a diner that leaves you with a tinge of sadness.

Yet, there was something about this word that wouldn't let go of me when writing this chapter. Out of pure curiosity,

I finally looked up the origin and I came across the Old English root "eall ān," literally meaning "wholly oneself."

To be "alone" wasn't about loneliness. It was about getting back to who I was when I first came on this earth. Alone, yet wholly oneself. It was as if the world had conspired with the powers that be to tell me just what I needed to hear, and now suddenly everything made sense.

Not everything I went after aligned with my own idea of a "good life." I had been climbing someone else's version of success, scaling the ladder of the American Dream. But at some point, the rungs grew too far apart and I couldn't avoid the widening gap that forced me to pause. Leaving me suspended in midair, wondering—after years of striving—what came next.

In Luke Burgis's book on mimetic desire, he articulates that our longing to imitate others—what he terms "metaphysical desire"—is an endless chase. We look to people as models believing they possess the key to fulfillment. Yet, the moment we find ourselves reaching for what they have, we move on to the next; as Burgis says, "we cycle through models faster than we cycle through clothes." This cycle of pursuit and dissatisfaction is like a bad game where winning feels like losing.

We're all being influenced in one way or another. Stories drive our lives, but it's only when we take time alone that we start to see which ones are driving ours. That's how we grow up. And I can honestly say it's some of the hardest work I've ever done.

And arguably the most freeing.

Stepping *into* Creativity

JUST AS SPORTS SERVE AS A MICROCOSM OF LIFE, athletes give us a glimpse of what it looks like to move through it with grit, creativity, and heart. The goal isn't to be like them—it's to be more like yourself.

An athlete isn't trying to be perfect. They can't be when the best of them miss more than half their shots or have batting averages under .300. I think, in part, that's why sports resonate so deeply across cultures.

Despite their best effort, the potential outcome is fraught with uncertainties and disappointments. We see

STEPPING INTO CREATIVITY

athletes who have no choice but to accept their weaknesses and show up regardless of them.

When we create, we send flares out to each other.

I've felt this firsthand when my palms start sweating watching my team try to win, diving into a book that articulates the things I've struggled to voice, or getting lost in a song that time-stamps a moment in my life. It's about showing parts of ourselves to the world—parts we once kept hidden.

That's the thing about creativity and inspiration—we often confuse them. We start by adopting the identities of those who inspire us, and while that's a great place to begin, we were never meant to stay there. Ideally, we move beyond inspiration, using their work as a guide to discover our own—to take what resonates, filter it through our own lens, and step into creating.

That's what the capsule wardrobe approach really taught me. It showed me that we're not meant to just consume beautiful things. Deep down, we all know how to create and be part of them. We just need the space, and the courage, to start.

Finding Pacesetters

I WAS COZIED UP IN A CHAIR IN THE CORNER OF A coffeehouse with a background hum of conversation filling the air. The aroma of freshly brewed coffee steamed from the warm mug in my hands. This space is one of my favorite places in the entire world. I am alone but surrounded by the unfolding of life around me.

I get the same feeling when I stay up late at night typing on my computer. There's something about knowing that while the whole house sleeps, I have space to hear my thoughts flow freely. Time seems to slow when I'm together, alone.

FINDING PACESETTERS

Being alone is like being plugged into a power source. It's where I find the energy that fully recharges me. Able to contribute far more to the people around me than when I'm running on empty.

Take, for instance, Nike's Breaking2 project. A group of runners attempted to break the two-hour marathon barrier, a feat never before accomplished. To do this, Nike selected three elite runners and established a highly controlled environment to optimize their performance. The main strategy was to use a team of world-class pacesetters, helping the main runners stay on track to break the two-hour barrier.

The pacesetters adopted a formation that shielded the three runners from the wind, providing an aerodynamic advantage. They alternated positions to remain fresh and maintain the desired pace. Throughout the race, they followed a lead car projecting a laser line on the ground, indicating the exact speed needed to complete the marathon in under two hours.

Ultimately, Eliud Kipchoge came closest to breaking the two-hour barrier, finishing the race in two hours and twenty-five seconds. Though the group didn't technically break the record, the event showcased the importance of pacesetters and collaboration in pushing an individual's performance beyond what people thought to be humanly possible. No one else can do the work for us or tell us what we need, but the people we surround ourselves with make the difference in determining what we are capable of.

It's said that we are the sum of the five people we spend the most time with. If there's truth in this, then choosing these individuals wisely is one of the most important decisions you'll ever make.

Time alone may recharge us, but having the right people by our side reminds us of who we are when we might otherwise feel lost.

Shifting *Gears*

IT WAS A FRIDAY AFTERNOON AT TWO O'CLOCK when I felt my blinks starting to slow, my eyelids weighing heavier. With a space heater at the bottom of my feet exactly how I like it—burning lava hot—I felt every muscle in my body begin to relax. I desperately wanted to take a nap.

Katie, my old college roommate, had come up days earlier to visit from Florida, and with years to catch up on, we put our senses aside and stayed up past midnight two nights in a row. It was as if we had reverted to our old college days. My late thirties were showing themselves in full force.

It wouldn't be the first time I had been tempted to curl up and sleep at two in the afternoon, but didn't actually do it. How could I? I couldn't think of a single story about a woman who took an afternoon nap and was still considered a success. Who did she become?

The guilt would inevitably scoot me away from the space heater and toward an afternoon coffee as fuel for lack of energy. What I couldn't do, a shot of espresso certainly could. I had spent years running on that kind of borrowed energy, pushing forward at a pace that wasn't mine, afraid to slow down, afraid to fall behind.

But this time was different.

This time, I felt the subtle shift—the course correction from the story I had inherited to the one I was in the process of rewriting. A story where success wasn't measured by how quickly I could keep up.

So instead of another espresso, I shut my eyes. And I took a nap.

Being *in* *the* Flow

I WAS ON THE CORNER OF THE COURT, BARELY IN bounds, fluorescent lights beaming on me, sweat dripping down the side of my face. The girl guarding me had given me enough space to shoot. I was too far out, a foot or so past the three-point line, but I decided to do it anyway. The ball left my hands all the way from downtown, with a slight height advantage over my defender. The ball went in.

Then again, and again.

And again. Until the other team finally caught on, I could have shot from anywhere that afternoon. Lights out with my eyes closed. I don't think it mattered. The ball was making its way to the goal. I ended with thirty-five points—holding the record for the highest single-scoring game in school history. It wasn't only that night. It continued to happen twice more when I was in college, two games each with seven three-pointers.

Time stopped ticking, temporarily suspended. I was no longer in my head. Any doubts or expectations melted away. Every move I made was with ease and effortlessness that stayed challenging for others. I hit one three-pointer after another, not fully knowing how but not questioning it, either. I was completely absorbed in the joy of playing.

In basketball, they call it being "in the flow." In daily life, I liken it to experiencing freedom—when you don't overthink and are fully yourself, getting a glimpse, if only for a second, of how simple and beautiful life can be.

It's contagious to everyone around.

PART FIVE

The Road Ahead

A Freer, More Beautiful Way to Live

> Do not go where the path may lead, go instead where there is no path and leave a trail.

—RALPH WALDO EMERSON

Crossing Mile One

I WAS ROUGHLY A HALF MILE IN WHEN I STARTED TO think, "This is the reason I never run."

Distance running has never been my forte. I always felt it was meant for "those other people" who enjoy torturing themselves for no apparent reason.

Nevertheless, armed with *Atomic Habits* as my guidebook and a new pair of shoes, I convinced myself I needed to fully embrace my newfound identity. I was ready.

Every day for a solid month, I'd tie my shoes and walk out the door, gradually turning my walk into a jog, attempting to trick my mind into believing we were runners. No matter how many times I ran, it didn't begin to feel easier until I hit mile one.

Every run would start the same—winded, achy, and tired. Then, like clockwork, a miracle would happen at the first-mile marker. I'd experience what can only be described as my legs moving without me telling them to and my breath settling into the new pace.

Suddenly, I was okay. Was it hard? Yes. But I finally felt at ease. My mind and body were no longer fighting what I was putting it through. Mile one turned into mile two, into mile three... Let's not get crazy. I'm no Mo Farah.

With running, we tend to talk much more about our victories at the finish line or starting a new habit than what happens in between.

Our culture is built around productivity and self-improvement, and it shows when books like *Atomic Habits* reign for a whopping nine months on *The New York Times* Best Seller list. We desperately want to be better humans, but the messiness of the middle can throw us off. So I was surprised when my brother-in-law (a veteran marathon runner) confirmed what I had long suspected.

"Mile one always sucks."

I won't claim that this affirmation turned me into a distance runner. It did, however, remind me of what I had long forgotten.

CROSSING MILE ONE

Everything in me wanted to stop running right before hitting mile one. Even as I write today, I can envision the wide turn on my route, crossing from one sidewalk to another. It's not lost on me that there was a stop sign that mirrored my inner dialogue. Stopping here would've meant enduring all the hard work of starting without reaping any of the benefits of the runner's high. No matter the season, the space after starting something new is always hard.

Everyone talks about how exciting it is to start a new job, habit, or adventure, but pushing past that initial phase—that's where the real challenge lies. It's the same with editing your life. At first, the change required to cut back, let go, or live with less can feel unnatural—like the first exhausting steps of a run. You can't judge the whole experience based on mile one.

When you give yourself enough grace to find your rhythm and choose to keep going, that's when everything starts to change.

Moving Through *the* Messy Middle

T HERE'S A LADY IN MY HOMETOWN WHO HAS HAD the same hairstyle since she was in high school. Now, you might think that's not all that strange. If you see it, the distinct poof of the permed bangs that could have only been perfected in the late '70s, you would think otherwise.

Even as a child, I was intrigued by how her hairstyle acted like a timestamp, marking the moment when the world seemed to move on without her. I don't know her full story;

this woman, with her enduring hairstyle, might have very well found her *chisoku*. It would be unfair for me to judge her merely by what I see on the surface, but it has made me think about the fine line between knowing who we are and staying in our comfort zone. It made me ask: Am I keeping things because I love them, or because I'm scared to let them go?

We all hang on to the familiar; after all, it's hard to step beyond our comfort zone, even when it no longer serves us. Even when going in a new direction, as terrifying as it feels, is what keeps us truly alive. As Brené Brown says, "The middle is messy, but it's also where the magic happens." And yet, when we reach that messy middle, where the old is gone but the new hasn't yet taken shape, it's easy to mistake discomfort for a sign that we're going the wrong way and should turn back.

We tell ourselves logical stories about why we shouldn't continue pursuing what's new:

"It's financially irresponsible."

"It's too risky."

"We're too far in, too old."

Sometimes, these concerns are valid. But too often, they become excuses that keep us from moving forward.

What we rarely talk about is the seductive comfort of the middle—call it middle age, middle class, or middle management. I've watched people reach this stage of life and start choosing comfort in the name of contentment, unaware that the trade-off they're making is the feeling of coming alive. The middle is where so many dreams go to die—not because people stop wanting more, but because they convince themselves they can't have it. It's where doubt settles in, where fear masquerades as logic. I've read countless self-help books that insist starting is the hardest part. But it's not. The real challenge is continuing after the excitement fades and uncertainty sets in. If we can stay in that tension, if we can resist the urge to settle, we give ourselves the greatest chance to build a life more beautiful than we ever imagined.

I always wondered how cranky old people who tip poorly turned into these hardened versions of themselves. Being smack-dab in the middle of my thirties is like having a front-row seat to the sliding door moments that make or break how many of us live the second half of our lives.

People who were once lively and spirited, with dreams they would have fought for in their twenties, turn into curmudgeons by the ripe old age of forty. I used to think that taking a big leap into the unknown was too daunting. Now, I see that the real fear was in letting go of what was comfortable.

I had experienced this feeling once before in my first closet cleanout. Anytime I felt a lack of direction, it was debilitating. Even basic inquiries or well-intentioned guidance could send me spiraling. Questions like "What do you want?" didn't help. I spent so much time thinking about all the possibilities and what I thought others expected that I didn't trust my own opinion to go rogue and create a new path for myself.

Change is hard. There is a real loss in letting go of the stories I once told myself, even when I know they are no longer what I want. For the longest time, I couldn't put a name to what I was experiencing. It was the discomfort of change but it was also grief. Grief of losing my old identity as an entrepreneur, as an athlete, of leaving behind the version of myself who believed I needed one more thing to solve my problem, or with a little hard work I could determine my outcome.

Change came with real trade-offs. I could reason all day about the benefits of taking the road less traveled, but it didn't stop culture from praising those who continued to chase after wealth, fame, power, and pleasure. Watching others receive praise for following these well-trodden paths didn't make sticking to my own any easier. The hardest part is resisting the urge to settle and instead choosing to live each day in alignment with the parts of myself, the essentials, I'd uncovered.

For this new lifestyle to take root, I had to stand on solid ground, rewrite my narrative, and recognize the extraordinary in what I once saw as ordinary. Maybe greatness was never about meeting society's definition—it was about defining it for myself. More than that, it was about living it fully.

Writing *a* New Story

CELEBRATED MY THIRTIETH BIRTHDAY WITH FIVE hundred strangers singing to me in New York City.

Let's back up.

A week earlier, I'd made plans to celebrate this milestone at a Seth Godin conference. Seth Godin is an author of twenty bestselling books and a renowned speaker, teacher, and entrepreneur. He's the godfather of marketing, known for encouraging others to "go and make a ruckus." He's a freaking legend.

Spending my thirtieth birthday at a Seth Godin conference revealed my dedication to learning about human behavior and my nerdy fandom.

Upon arrival, every attendee, including my husband, was given a playing card. The two people at the conference who were given aces would go home with a Seth Godin limited edition book—a compilation of his most recent written works, weighing eighteen pounds.

When we realized my husband was one of the lucky winners, we felt it was a kind of birthday charm. At intermission, we got in line to meet Seth and have him sign our eighteen-pound book.

When we got to the front, my husband told Seth how great it was that we won because we were there celebrating my thirtieth birthday. He graciously said, "Happy Birthday," and signed the book. Off we went, nerding out and thrilled to have met him in person.

An hour later, in the second half of the conference, Seth diverted from his onstage story to ask, "Is Erin in the audience?" Like everyone else, I began looking around for the Erin he was speaking to. He clarified by saying, "Erin, with the thirtieth birthday."

I froze. My eyes frantically scanned the room until it sunk in that he was talking about me. I slowly inched my hand in the air. Once he spotted my hand creeping up, he nodded with a confirmation look.

Seth directed the entire audience of five hundred attendees to sing "Happy Birthday." They obliged and sang loudly as I nervously smiled back at the crowd. Being sung at by a large group of close-sitting strangers is an awkward phenomenon. The energy was palpable. I sat in disbelief that every person in the conference, including the person I came to see, was staring and singing at me.

As it ended, I took a deep breath, my cheeks hurting from the intense smile on my face. Without hesitation, Seth said, "Let's do it again!"

"This time, I want you to sing with all your heart as if Erin is the best and closest friend you've ever had. Sing as if you came here to New York City to celebrate her. Shout it to the rooftops!"

He upped the ante. They accepted the challenge by erupting in chorus.

Five hundred people, some standing on chairs, raised their hands like conductors and sang with all their might. I soaked in every note. I felt the abundance of love from complete and utter strangers, Seth himself. I'm not sure I've ever experienced such delight.

Once it ended, he addressed the crowd: "This, she will never forget. The first time you sang, it made for a great story. The second time you sang, it changed her, and you, too, were better for it."

The point he was trying to make was clear as day: If you want to be remarkable, do something worth remarking on.

It doesn't take more time or money, just the willingness to step off the beaten path. That is all.

He was right. I can't remember last year's birthday, but I can tell you this story like it was yesterday. Remarkable lives aren't built by following the script. They take shape when we stop doing what we're supposed to and start moving into uncharted territory. Because that's where we show up as ourselves. Where we peel off the layers we've been hiding behind.

That's where real connection is found, not in the certainty of the well-worn path, but in the honesty of the unknown.

Staying Grounded

THE STORIES THAT WERE DRIVING MY LIFE weren't for nothing. They helped me accomplish much of what I wouldn't trade. But now I see that much of what I've achieved could have been filled with less stress, striving, and pain.

There were times when my opinion was buried beneath the opinions of others—coaches, investors, bosses, friends, and family. Now I can't help but wonder how things might have been different. How many messy, beautiful moments did I overlook along the way?

It's funny how easy it is to miss what's right in front of you. If you've ever been to Cincinnati, you'd know the trees are hard to miss. Set on the Ohio River, small forests and hills give deer enough courage to roam wildly in the city. Yet, for years, I barely noticed them.

I felt the weather shift from warm to cool for nearly a decade, but I couldn't have told you when the trees' leaves went from full to bare. It was as if it happened all of a sudden. Seasons of life would literally pass me by without my ever pausing to notice the present.

Fast-forward to today. I feel joy when leaves sprout or turn from vibrant green to soft yellow. In some ways, I swung the pendulum too far, as my husband would note by my obsession with crushing acorns on our walks. It looks like I've been day drinking with all the meandering. That's the thing: My daily walks are for wandering and acorn-crushing, looking up at the sky and noticing which trees keep their leaves longer and which turn specific colors for only two weeks a year. They are everyday, seemingly mundane moments that mark the passage of time.

I feel this most when I go to the beach.

In true Midwestern fashion, my family would opt to drive the ten-plus hours in the car, making the necessary pit stops at the "good" gas stations along the way. Still, to this day, when flying could get us to the sandy shores in less than three hours, we choose to drive. There's something about the long travel from point A to point B that allows me to decompress, switching modes from "always on" to "vacation." There are very few places I'd rather be than the beach. The vast ocean instills a sense of calm within me, and I'm always struck by how powerful it looks and how small I feel in its presence.

When we arrive, no matter the condo we rent, I am reminded of a terrifying (yet effective) magnet stuck to the front of the refrigerator warning of rip currents. Every vacation, I passed by this magnet, never giving it much thought. Something about this trip—about the stillness and distance from my daily life—made me see that warning in a new light.

Culture is a rip current.

It pulls at us subtly, slowly, without force. One moment, we're simply going about our lives, getting A's on the honor roll, securing the promotion followed by a raise for our hard work, and checking off the milestones: marriage, house, kids. And then suddenly, we look up and realize just how far we've drifted from who we thought we were.

Even the smartest among us struggle with change because it can feel like our very identity is at stake. When your sense of self is anchored to a belief, a career, a political stance, or a public persona, any questioning can feel like losing a part of yourself. The more publicly you've declared something—whether on social media or around the dinner table—the harder it becomes to step back, reassess, and work through the discomfort that leads to real growth.

But if your identity is rooted in something unshakable—God, truth, deeper values—then change is not as threatening when you already know where you stand.

The real question is: Where are your feet planted?

If your sense of self is built on success, money, reputation, or power, sooner or later, the ground beneath you is going to shift. And when it does, you start to realize just how much you've been holding on to things that were never meant to hold you up in the first place. For so long, I thought the answer was to push harder—to prove myself, to earn my place, to fight my way back to some version of success that would keep me safe. But the harder I fought, the more exhausted I became. You don't escape a rip current by sheer effort. You escape by surrendering to a different way.

The real security didn't come from striving for more: clothes, money, or respect. It came when I loosened my grip, stopped resisting, and let go of the version of myself I thought I had to be. That's when everything changed. That's when I saw it clearly—sometimes, the way forward isn't about pushing through. It's about learning to swim sideways, trusting that solid ground is still there, waiting for you.

Slowing down became a practice, not a luxury. And the beach was where I learned to do it best. I wander through the sand, unhurried, with nothing but the sun to mark the passing of time. I wake up without an alarm and grab a coffee while sitting on the deck. Then, I move to the oceanfront, where my chair rotates like clockwork. Returning to the condo for lunch, then back out again. When I inevitably face the west, I know it's time to go up for the day. There's no rushing about, just the breeze and the wind—the much-needed break before I head back home to my usual routine.

Time has a way of standing still at the beach, neither hurried nor lagging. It's as if each second is exactly where it's meant to be, unfolding naturally. In recent years, I've come to think that vacations are not an escape from reality but a call to it. A natural pace that, in a matter of a week's time, magically reminds us of what's essential. It's as if this is how we were supposed to live all along. As author Annie Dillard wisely observed, "How we spend our days is, of course, how we spend our lives."

These days, living differently feels like stepping outside the pace and norms of our culture in the smallest, everyday ways. Repeating outfits and walking are two things that bring me a sense of calm. It might seem insignificant, but in a way, dressing for myself has felt a lot like writing this book—learning to put words to the feelings I once kept hidden.

I'm sharing these stories not for approval, but in hopes that someone else might relate to them. Because connection, the real kind, happens when we let ourselves be seen as we are.

And when we stop chasing, stop performing—when we stand still long enough to actually be where our feet are—that's when we finally step onto the road less worn.

AFTERWORD
Your Compass

The pause between Christmas and New Year's, when the world moves at a pace where I can finally catch my breath, is one of my favorite times of the year. This year, though, it felt different. A restlessness stirred within me. So I gave myself a challenge: read for five minutes before bed. Those five minutes turned into a morning ritual, and soon, piles of books were scattered around my house. Reading the stories of others gave me words to articulate my own. Words I had silenced.

After a decade of writing nothing beyond occasional blog articles, I hit a tipping point. Initially, I was hesitant to jot down notes on my phone, not because I feared others' judgments—no one else would see them—but because I was terrified of confronting my own. This wasn't the first time I'd avoided my feelings. My once-overstuffed closet was a testament to how I tried to shop my way out of them.

Long before I had the idea of writing a book, I barely allowed myself to revisit the past. The stories I remembered left me uneasy, tangled in blame, guilt, and shame. Writing caught me by surprise. Rather than reinforcing my old views, I found compassion for those I had labeled as villains and beauty in the hard places I had tried to forget.

After everyone went to bed, I stayed awake. Slipping into the office next to my bedroom, I typed. Words flooded out of me. The first story I wrote down was about my so-called "friend" from earlier chapters who, over a basket of chicken wings at Buffalo Wild Wings, casually mentioned that women were too emotional to run a company. Then I described my second-grade classroom and how I'd challenge the boys on the playground. Each memory, now captured in text, revealed more than the glow of my screen. There was a narrative about proving, belonging, and hard work—stories that shaped who I thought I needed to be as a woman, an athlete, and an entrepreneur. Writing it down brought me to a new place. It showed me so many of the reasons why I felt like I couldn't be myself.

AFTERWORD

How striving, often for approval, only reinforced what I thought I was missing.

Then, one day, I began putting together a capsule wardrobe. It was like holding up a mirror to my life. As if I had been trying to fill a cup with a gaping hole in the side—that was the story I'd told myself. The overflowing clothes told a different one. There was no leak. Everything I needed, I already had.

How I approached my wardrobe reshaped not only my style but also my sense of self. The way I live, how I work, what I eat, and the way I interact with friends. This idea that clutter was the very thing making life more complicated sounds straightforward now, but starting with what I love, not what I lack, marked a life-altering shift in my perspective.

There might be more efficient ways to write a book, yet the way each part unfolded—seemingly without any order—led me to answer the question I posed at the start: "How did I end up here?"

I spent much of my life giving others what I needed to offer myself: love, trust, and acceptance. As it turns out, being known is not the same as being loved.

This path hasn't been without its challenges or the occasional pain that comes from missing out on what's considered "normal." Now, I can see the stories for what they are.

I've found a steadiness in knowing that the paths others follow, as lovely as they may be, were never meant for me.

My hope is in traveling down the road less worn I may leave a trail for someone else. And my capsule wardrobe? Well, that's my compass.

It keeps guiding me back to who I am when I occasionally get lost.

I needed that sense of direction more than ever on a warm fall afternoon, just days before Halloween, as I took a call from a book agent.

Throughout my writing process, I'd been cautioned that publishing was its own beast, with unspoken rules, rhythms, and a list of "shoulds" to follow. "It's been done like this for years," they'd say. Who was I to argue with an industry that had produced countless books now stacked in the cozy corner of my kitchen or piled as high as the lamp by my bed? These traditionally published works, loved by me and many others, have left indelible marks on my life—each shaping the direction I've taken.

In the early days of writing, I deliberately ignored the publishing process until my book was complete. It felt like running a marathon, with my only goal being to cross the finish line. There was no "26.2" bumper sticker for this achievement, just a manuscript with a title and a home in my Google Docs. Once the pages were done, I

AFTERWORD

lifted my head and began the journey to get published. I braced myself, expecting an experience much like pitching a startup to a venture capitalist—one side holding all the power, and my job being to sell a vision. I hoped that this time, I could stomach it.

After a few technical issues with Zoom, she called me, and we began talking. It had been a while since I'd spoken about myself out loud, but I was ready to discuss the book and share my background. She started by asking about Cladwell, so I recounted the story of its creation. Then, her questions became more pointed, zeroing in on my platform: Instagram following, subscriber count, demographics. Thrown off, I rattled off stats, emphasizing our loyal user base. As we neared the thirty-minute mark, it became clear that this conversation wasn't about who I was or the chapters I'd poured the last two years into. Content was no longer king; it had been dethroned by Instagram and TikTok. Influencers were the new royalty, and a large, dedicated audience was now the crown jewel.

Her advice: build a dedicated following. Then, we'll talk. We ended the call, and I felt the ick—not at her, as she was doing her job, but at the world we live in.

I couldn't help but think: If I took this advice to heart, the "smart" parenting move would be to teach my son how to play the game. I'd encourage him, early and often, to dedicate time to social media, curating a life that draws others in and persuades them to follow his. Do it authentically, of course—in a way that gains an audience ready to buy when it's time to sell, allowing him to unlock doors that I couldn't.

But I don't want that for him.

I want my son to find joy in creating, to understand the value of putting in honest work to hone his craft and practice his skills. I want him to pursue becoming the best version of himself and experience the deep connection that comes from sharing who he really is with those around him. And when the world comes knocking, asking him to do more, I want him to have the strength to say no.

I don't think Jesus was being rhetorical when he asked, "For what will it profit a man if he gains the whole world and forfeits his soul?"

And what price are we willing to pay to chase what we want?

I once heard someone say you don't truly know your values until you realize what you're unwilling to compromise. Writing this book made it clear to me: There is no goal, no matter how impressive or altruistic it may appear, worth trading my soul for.

Two years ago, I would have chased those elusive keys, fighting relentlessly until I was worn out, blaming myself

AFTERWORD

for not being good enough to get past the gatekeepers. Even if I'd succeeded, expecting validation as a published author, I know now it would come with the pressure to achieve more. A bigger publisher, a better-selling book. I've been down this road before, setting my sights on the mountain top only to feel the pressure to reach another peak.

If writing has lost its art, we owe it to ourselves to stop the charades. It's not that every published writer today lacks talent, yet being a nonfiction writer now also means being an influencer—a requirement that feels misplaced. I've seen enough to know I can't decide the right path for anyone else, but I do know this—something about it isn't right for me.

When I was twenty-two and fresh out of college, struggling to find a job, I came across an ebook by Charlie Hoehn. His story was so much like mine: a recent graduate caught in the uncertainty of an economic downturn. Reading his words felt like having a conversation with a friend who had been there, too. It took away the shame of feeling like I was the only millennial facing an uphill battle.

That little, self-published book changed my life. Instead of spending my days glued to job boards, hoping for a hiring manager to notice me, his story gave me permission to ignore the script about what the critics said was "best" and take a different route.

Maybe choosing the indie path to publish my book was some final test. Was I really willing to let go of what others thought of me? Could I forgo the clout of saying I'd been traditionally published?

The call didn't go as I'd originally hoped. But it felt like fate nonetheless. I can't help but see the irony in realizing the punch line of the whole book only after I thought I had it all wrapped up in a pretty bow. I had hoped this time pitching would be different. As it turns out, it was.

I was.

THE JOURNEY
by **MARY OLIVER**

One day you finally knew
what you had to do, and began,
though the voices around you
kept shouting
their bad advice—
though the whole house
began to tremble
and you felt the old tug
at your ankles.
"Mend my life!"
each voice cried.
But you didn't stop.
You knew what you had to do,
though the wind pried
with its stiff fingers
at the very foundations,

though their melancholy
was terrible.
It was already late
enough, and a wild night,
and the road full of fallen
branches and stones.
But little by little,
as you left their voices behind,
the stars began to burn
through the sheets of clouds,
and there was a new voice
which you slowly
recognized as your own,
that kept you company
as you strode deeper and deeper
into the world,
determined to do
the only thing you could do—
determined to save
the only life you could save.

ACKNOWLEDGMENTS

For years, I've listened to authors on podcasts talk about the painstaking process of writing a book. I used to think their stories were a bit exaggerated. How hard could it really be to write down your own story?

Well, the joke's on me—ten times over. Trying to capture the swirling thoughts in my head and the messy beauty of lived experiences on paper has felt like trying to lasso a raging bull. Writing these words in black and white, in a way another human might make sense of them, required nothing short of a small village.

Michella: Without you, this book would have stayed a messy first draft. Thank you for not only being a supportive sister but also taking precious time out of your already-full schedule to read it line by line.

Amy: You are the editor every aspiring writer dreams of. I'm so lucky to call you my friend. You made this book better—full stop.

Sara: For every time I talked about writing this book and every moment you showed up with the kind of friendship I needed—thank you.

Laura: You've been the friend I could bring every insecurity to, knowing they'd be held safely. You gave me the fuel I needed to get to the finish line.

Friyay Friends (Arian, Robbie, Krissy, Jonathan, Justin, Dan, and Kyle): There aren't enough words to describe the endless support, patience, and coffee you've given me week after week to help me bring my creative projects to life. "Lucky" doesn't even begin to cover how I feel about having you all in my life.

Mom and Dad: This relationship isn't balanced—I'm the one who benefits tenfold. You've always believed in me, no matter the turn I take. This time was no different.

Tony: You're the brother who supports every crazy idea I pursue. Ready to "buy it" no matter what I'm working on.

Christine, Andrea, and Kacy: This book is a result of your time and investment. I don't take that lightly—thank you.

Rooney: Thank you for being patient when my laptop was open at all the wrong times. When I told you I was writing a book, you said, "That's so good, Mama." It was everything I needed to hear.

Colin: Last but not least, thank you to the one who heard a dream and never once discouraged it. For nearly

ACKNOWLEDGMENTS

three years, you gave me the time, space, and unwavering support to bring this book to life. This book is possible because of you.

ABOUT THE AUTHOR

Erin Flynn is the CEO and founder of Cladwell, the leading smart closet and daily outfit app with over one million downloads. Her career has spanned the worlds of fashion, tech, and entrepreneurship, taking her from the heart of influencer culture to cofounding startups and now to writing a memoir that reveals the emotional and personal insights gained along the way.

She participated in top accelerator programs like 500 Global and Indie.VC, and raised venture capital—all while feeling the pressures of both the fashion and tech worlds up close. Today, through Cladwell, Erin helps people rethink how they approach their closets, encouraging a more thoughtful and sustainable way of getting dressed. Her path—from college athletics to fashion to startups, and ultimately, self-discovery—has inspired her to share her story in a way that feels deeply personal and true.

Erin knows firsthand that creating a life you love requires intentionality, often taking big steps back to move forward. She's experienced firsthand the burnout and moments when the light dims. While many people share curated versions of their experiences on social media, Erin sees a gap when it comes to being vulnerable about the emotional journey. The few truly honest conversations she's had with other creatives have left her feeling more refreshed and connected—and less alone in the daunting task of building a life you love.

With only 2 percent of women founders receiving funding, that feeling of loneliness is not just emotional—it's a reality. As one of the few women who have been in the startup space, Erin believes it's more important than ever to speak up and share her story. After years of collecting experiences, she feels compelled to tell them.

Through her unfiltered lens, she discovers that success isn't a silver bullet, progress doesn't follow a straight line, and building a life we love doesn't always come from taking the biggest leaps. Instead, it's often found when we give ourselves what we offer to others: love, trust, and acceptance.

ABOUT *Cladwell*

Cladwell is a leading daily outfit and smart closet app that transforms the way people interact with their wardrobes. With over one million downloads, Cladwell digitizes your closet and helps you uncover the pieces you love, curate them to mix and match, and define your unique style—making getting dressed effortless.

Thousands of people use Cladwell every day to build wardrobes they love and actually wear. The app has cataloged over 13 million items, recommended over 100 million outfits, and successfully dressed users 3.5 million times. By introducing users to the capsule wardrobe approach, Cladwell reduces decision fatigue, helps others have sustainable style, and eliminates the constant need for new purchases.

Rooted in a mission to simplify and personalize style, Cladwell believes in style for good. Today's fast-fashion culture results in excessive waste, with an average of eighty pounds of clothing discarded per person each year. Cladwell challenges this "more is better" mindset by making it fun to buy less, wear more, and make intentional fashion choices that are better for people and the planet.

More than just an app, Cladwell is a movement. It's proof that there's a smarter, more sustainable approach to fashion—helping you love your wardrobe while shaping a better future for you and the place we call home.

To learn more, visit *cladwell.com*.

Download the Cladwell app *for free* via the App Store or on Google Play.

To learn more about the capsule wardrobe, take the Capsule Wardrobe Course *for free* at *cladwell.com/capsule-wardrobe-program*.